Beginning Old Testament Study

Beginning Old Testament Study

Edited by John Rogerson

The Westminster Press
Philadelphia

The authors retain the copyright of their contributions
© John Rogerson   David J. A. Clines   Paul Joyce   John Barton 1982

Published by The Westminster Press®
Philadelphia, Pennsylvania

Printed in the United States of America
9 8 7 6 5 4 3 2 1

Library of Congress Cataloging in Publication Data

Main entry under title:

Beginning Old Testament study.

   Includes index.
   1. Bible. O.T.—Criticism, interpretation, etc.—
Addresses, essays, lectures. 2. Bible. O.T.—Study—
Addresses, essays, lectures. I. Rogerson, J.W.
(John William), 1935–
BS1192.B37 1982   221.6′1   82-20210
ISBN 0-664-24451-3 (pbk.)

Contents

66797

The Contributors

JOHN ROGERSON is Professor and Head of the Department of Biblical Studies at the University of Sheffield. He is also an Honorary Canon of Sheffield Cathedral. His published works include *Myth in Old Testament Interpretation* (1974), *The Supernatural in the Old Testament* (1976), *Psalms* (1977) with J. W. McKay, and *Anthropology and the Old Testament* (1978).

JOHN BARTON is Fellow and Chaplain of St Cross College, Oxford, and Lecturer in Theology (Old Testament) at the University of Oxford. He is the author of *Amos's Oracles Against the Nations* (1980), and a contributor to *Believing in the Church* (1981), the report by the Doctrine Commission of the Church of England, of which he is a member.

DAVID J. A. CLINES is Reader in Biblical Studies at the University of Sheffield, and a member of the Christian Brethren. His previous books are *I, He, We and They: A Literary Approach to Isaiah 53* (1976), *The Theme of the Pentateuch* (1979), and *Art and Meaning: Rhetoric in Biblical Literature* (1982), of which he is a joint editor.

PAUL JOYCE is a Roman Catholic layman on the staff of Ripon College, Cuddesdon, Oxford. A former Kennicott Hebrew Fellow at the University of Oxford, he has made a particular study of the Old Testament prophets.

Introduction

On any showing, the Old Testament is a remarkable collection of books produced by a remarkable group of people. Except for several brief spells when they ruled over small neighbouring peoples, the ancient Israelites were not a military or political force to be reckoned with. They lived at the edge of the main international route from Egypt to northern Mesopotamia, and for much of their history they struggled to retain their identity in the face of the imperialistic expansions of Egypt, Assyria, Babylon, Persia, the Hellenistic successors of Alexander the Great, and Rome. On several occasions, they retained their separate identity at the expense of becoming vassal states. In 721 BC, the Assyrians brought to an end the separate national existence of the ten tribes which had formed the northern kingdom since Solomon's death. In 587 BC, the Babylonians brought to an end the southern kingdom of Judah. The temple in Jerusalem was destroyed, and the city itself was sacked. The most prominent of the people were taken off to exile in Babylon, there to join a larger number of exiles from Judah who had been deported on the occasion of the first great Babylonian victory in 597.

The loss of Jerusalem and of the temple in 587 ought to have brought to an end the separate existence of the ancient Israelites. They ought to have disappeared like their neighbours Ammon, Edom, Moab and the Philistines, leaving behind only traces that the archaeologists would discover 2,500 years later. But they did not cease to exist. Characteristically, a prophetic group among the exiles took up and enlarged the theme of the preaching of Jeremiah at the time of Jerusalem's fall—that this fall was God's punishment of his people because of their persistent disloyalty. The exile became a time for positive reflection upon the past, and for the discovery of the value of suffering. The exiles looked forward in hope to a new beginning, a hope partially satisfied when, in 540, the Persian king Cyrus allowed some exiles to return to Jerusalem and to rebuild the temple.

1

This remarkable story of a people that refused to die is told in the Old Testament. But just as remarkable is the way in which it is told. It is true that the Old Testament contains sections in which the achievements of the Israelites are proudly presented. The section in 1 Kings 3—10 about Solomon and all his glory springs readily to mind. But on the whole, the story of the ancient Israelites is told not in order to glorify their achievements, but rather to emphasize their persistent disloyalty to God. The record is highly critical, and few kings, for example, escape without censure. Even David, who came in later Old Testament times to be regarded as a model king, is spared nothing as 2 Samuel 9—20 deals with his adultery with Bathsheba, his disposal of her husband, and the subsequent breakdown of relationships within his own family.

The criticism of Israel which runs through the Old Testament is an important clue to its origin and purpose. It is not the national literature of the ancient Israelite people. It is a collection of religious books, and it is probably the work of a smallish group who, generation after generation, bore witness to faith in God, often in the face of official disapproval, persecution, and even death.

One way of characterizing the Old Testament is to describe it as the story of the struggle between the God of Israel and the God of the Old Testament. The God of Israel was the god that the people wanted for their own convenience—a god who would win their battles, cure their illnesses, and look after their general well-being. After all, did not the old stories tell of how he had defeated the Egyptians and rescued the people from slavery? But this view of God was constantly challenged by those we may call the servants of the God of the Old Testament. They proclaimed that Israel existed to be the servant of God, and not vice versa. They pointed out the injustices done to the poor and the defenceless. They denounced the attempts of rulers and people alike to confuse God with the gods of other peoples. They stressed the implications of their belief that God was the sovereign lord of heaven and earth, and that it was his purpose to bless all the nations by establishing his universal rule. Those who proclaimed thus, did so because their encounter with their God left them no option.

The story of Israel, told critically by those who proclaimed God's wider purposes for mankind, can be found in parts of the Pentateuch (Genesis—Deuteronomy) and above all in what are known as the former prophets (Joshua—2 Kings). The latter prophets (Isaiah—Malachi) provide a prophetic companion to that story. However, the Old Testament contains much other material. In the books of Job and Ecclesiastes are to be found two of the most frank and penetrating explorations of the problems of suffering and doubt in any religious literature. The Psalms constitute a treasury of texts for use in worship, whether public or private, and frankly express the doubts, sufferings and anger of their authors, as well as great sentiments about faith and hope in God.

In many ways, the Old Testament is a remarkably contemporary book. Its writers were familiar with the tides of war rolling across a continent first one way, and then the other, as this century has seen it on the continent of Europe. The future often seemed threatening. Starvation through famine or pestilence, death through epidemics, loss of livelihood, suffering and injustice, were not unknown. The writers of the Old Testament had no more reason for hoping in the victory of the purposes of God than we have today, yet they persisted in their hope, and they survived. Again, parallels can be drawn between the Church and Israel as the people of God. In a nominally Christian country, there is a struggle between the conventional or 'folk' religion of the majority, and a witness of the minority that sometimes brings them into conflict with the majority. The history of the Church shows it to have been in many ways as faithless to God as was ancient Israel, and constantly in need of prophetic renewal.

If the Old Testament contains a remarkable story remarkably told, if it is frank about doubt and unjustified suffering, if it is a book of hope written from situations no more favourable to hope than our present world seems to be, it might be expected that Old Testament courses would be among the most interesting and exciting in college and university curricula. Yet this does not seem to be the case. From many quarters the complaint is heard that students entering higher education come with very low expectations about the value of Old Testament study, and that their attitude is not altered by their courses. Among the reasons for this may be ignorance of the content of the Old Testament, something which is very noticeable in present-day students. For many years now, schools and even Sunday schools have given up any attempt to provide pupils with a knowledge of the content of the Bible. Even regular worshippers in the Church of England, the present writer's own church, will be lucky to hear an Old Testament lesson regularly at the Parish

Communion, and a sermon on the Old Testament will be a rarity. The Old Testament has become largely unknown, even to many worshippers.

But the fault does not lie entirely with schools and churches. In colleges and universities, we have taken too much for granted. We have confronted our students not only with an unfamiliar text, but with unfamiliar methods by which to study it. We have assumed too easily that students would appreciate the difference between the academic study of the Old Testament, and its use in worship and evangelism. We have overlooked the fact that almost all of our students have a New Testament orientation, and that they look back to the Old Testament as preparation, anticipation or background for the New Testament. OT teachers, on the other hand, often see the matter differently. For them, especially if, like the authors of this book, they are practising Christians, the OT can, and must, stand on its own feet. While it may be incomplete, and thus find its completion in the NT, it is an expression arising from many concrete situations over many hundreds of years, of faith in the living God.

The essays that follow this introduction are not intended as a guide to the content of the Old Testament, but rather as a guide to how to approach the academic study of the OT. The opening chapter provides a brief account of the history of OT study, so as to enable beginners to appreciate more readily the nature of academic as opposed to other approaches. The second chapter deals with the so-called literary methods in OT study. For over two hundred years, scholars have investigated the possible sources used by the biblical writers, and the manner in which these sources were combined together. Yet it is the text as we have it that must always remain the basis of interpretation, and chapter 2 provides guidelines both for interpreting Old Testament literature and for relating the various literary methods to this end.

There follows a chapter about the historical traditions in the OT. What is the purpose of these traditions, how do they compare with modern scholarly reconstructions of ancient Israel's history, and what happens if the modern scholar feels it necessary to 'correct' the account presented in the OT? These are the main questions here. Chapter 4 sketches some of the cultural differences between the OT world and the contemporary world. These differences are not so great that we can only understand the OT if we read it with a special kind of cultural spectacles. On the other hand, at some points we can appreciate it more readily if we make some cultural adjustments to our approach.

In the second half of the book there is a deliberate shift to some of the theological problems encountered in OT study. The chapters on Old Testament Theology and on Ethics touch on some of the most difficult questions. For many people, the ethics of the OT are those of a primitive or barbaric tribe, while if the OT is to provide material for theology, at best it is a record of man's search for God, small parts of which almost reflect the spirit of the NT. While not shirking the difficulties, our chapters seek a more positive approach, and try to dispel some of the popular 'myths' about the OT.

The same is true of the chapters about the Individual and the Community, and the Relation of the OT to the NT. The first of these is concerned particularly with justice and punishment, and shows how the tension between individual responsibility and the corporate consequences of wrongdoing runs throughout the OT. The final chapter discusses and dismisses the view that the OT has no place in the Church, that the OT is about wrath and the NT is about love, and that we must interpret the OT today in the manner in which it was interpreted in NT times. An Epilogue discusses the contemporary use of the OT.

The present book may be likened to a travel guide. Its purpose is to illumine the academic study of the OT, so that both the study, and the OT itself, are better appreciated. It aims to help you over some of the first hurdles rather than to tell you everything that you will need to know by the time you have completed your studies. It is the hope of the authors that you will come to regard the OT as something exciting, something deserving the most serious study, and something whose challenge to mankind is by no means exhausted.

1

An Outline of the History of Old Testament Study

JOHN ROGERSON

Everyone is born into particular cultural and historical circumstances. If you were born twenty years ago, you will be familiar with television, manned flights to the moon, and inflation. If you had been born sixty-five years ago, by the time you were twenty you might have seen a television, you could not have expected that man would travel to the moon in your lifetime, and you would not have been bothered by inflation. If you had been growing up just before the Second World War, you would have been aware of quite different international problems compared with today. Then, there was no oil crisis, and no iron curtain dividing Europe into East and West.

We have no control over the cultural and historical circumstances in which we find ourselves before we reach adulthood; but we learn to live with them, and we come to terms with them. The same is true when you begin academic studies. You have no control over the burning issues and the favoured solutions that dominate a subject at the point of time when you begin your studies. Yet you have to come to terms with these burning issues and what are thought to be their most likely solutions.

There is, however, a difference between how we are affected by the general circumstances in which we grow up, and how we find an academic discipline when we enter it. We cannot easily escape from the general circumstances of life. In an age of saturation coverage of news, they are all too familiar. What has been happening in academic study is, however, quite unfamiliar to us. When we begin academic study, we may well be amazed at what the burning issues are. They may concern questions that we have never thought of, and which we cannot even fully understand.

In the case of Old Testament study there is an additional

difficulty. If we have any familiarity with the Old Testament, we have almost certainly got this either from church or school. There is the possibility that we have learned to think about the Old Testament in ways which will not be helpful for academic study. We may have been taught to accept everything that the Old Testament says at its face value, so that it will come as a shock to discover that academic study subjects the Old Testament to close and critical scrutiny. Or we may have been taught that the Old Testament is the record of man's search for God before the coming of Christ. As a result, we may find it hard to believe that the Old Testament contains anything of permanent religious significance. We may also have learned some false ideas about the history of critical biblical scholarship. For example, we might think that critical scholarship is something essentially recent, perhaps the result of theologians giving in to scientists after the publication of Darwin's *Origin of Species* in 1859, whereas before the nineteenth century, Christian scholars were never concerned with critical questions.

In our ordinary lives, even a superficial study of the history of how circumstances have come to be as they are, can help us to understand, and in some cases to react positively to, the situation in which we find ourselves. This is also true in regard to academic study in general, and to Old Testament study in particular. We may find it much easier to come to terms with critical scholarship if we know something about its history. The outline that will be presented in the remainder of this chapter will be highly selective. It will have the following aims. First, to show that in one sense of the word critical, Old Testament scholarship has always been critical. Second, I shall try to show what was the really new factor that emerged with the historical-critical method in the late eighteenth century. Third, I shall try to place modern fundamentalism in the context of this brief historical sketch, and try to explain why clashes between fundamentalism and critical scholarship still occur.

A   *Critical Scholarship before the Reformation*

In 1 Samuel 13.1, the traditional Hebrew text literally translated reads: 'Saul was one year old when he began to reign, and he reigned two years over Israel.'[1] The earliest translators and commentators on this passage could have said if they so wished, 'with God, all things are possible. It seems incredible that a man could become a king and commander at the age of one; but this is what the Scripture says, and we must accept it, lest we imply that God is a liar.' Perhaps some very early scholars did say this. What we know, however, is that there were scholars who realized that there was a difficulty. Not only did the verse contradict what is known about human growth and development; it contradicted other passages about the life of Saul in 1 Samuel. Thus the difficulty was solved in one of three ways. In the ancient Greek translations of the Old Testament, the earliest of which goes back to pre-Christian times, the verse is either omitted entirely, or a figure such as thirty is given. Ancient Jewish interpretation, which is reflected in the Authorized Version of the Bible (1611), produced sense by doing violence to Hebrew usage. The AV has, 'Saul reigned one year; and when he had reigned two years over Israel, Saul chose him three thousand men . . .' We have here good examples of critical scholarship. Faced with a passage which contradicted reason and the evidence of other passages, ways were found of getting sense out of the verse. Of the three solutions mentioned, the one nearest to the truth was probably that which assumed that a number had been lost, and which provided it by guesswork.

A remarkable piece of critical scholarship in the early Christian centuries was concerned to help establish the correct text of the Old Testament. The Old Testament is sometimes quoted in the New Testament with significant differences from the text of the Old Testament as we have it. A good example is the quotation of Amos 9.11–12 in Acts 15.16–18. Amos 9.12 reads (RSV):

> that they may possess the remnant of Edom
> and all the nations who are called by my name,
> says the LORD who does this.

Acts 15.17–18 cites the verse as follows:

> that the rest of men may seek the Lord,
> and all the Gentiles who are called by my name,
> says the Lord, who has made these things known from of old.

Such differences must have been worrying to early Christian scholars, quite apart from the fact that Jewish apologists accused Christians of falsifying the text of the Old Testament, while

Christians returned the accusation. In an attempt to provide the information on the basis of which the correct text of the Old Testament could be established, Origen compiled his *Hexapla.*

Origen (AD 185–245) lived in Caesarea, and had a patron who provided him with ample secretarial assistance. The *Hexapla* was an edition of the Old Testament in which the text was set out in six main parallel columns. The first column contained the Hebrew text, the second transliterated this into Greek, while the remaining columns contained translations of the Old Testament into Greek. The work was over 6,000 pages long, and survived until the Moslem invasions of the seventh century. It is known today only from quotations in the works of scholars who consulted it.

Two examples of critical scholarship in the fourth century are provided by the work of Eusebius of Caesarea, and Jerome. Eusebius compiled an *Onomasticon,* which was an attempt to identify the places mentioned in the Bible. He drew upon the work of earlier writers, as well as on his own knowledge of the land of the Bible. Jerome, who lived in Bethlehem, was the greatest Christian Hebrew scholar in the early Church. At a time when there were no Hebrew grammars, dictionaries or concordances, he learned Hebrew from local Jews sufficiently well to enable him to translate the Old Testament from Hebrew into Latin. He also wrote commentaries and treatises on the Old Testament, and for many centuries his work provided Christian scholars with most of their knowledge about the Hebrew of the Old Testament.

The critical scholarship so far described has demonstrated only the desire to establish so far as possible the most correct text of the Old Testament, and the wish to gain mastery over the main language in which it was written. Early critical scholarship was also facing up to questions that we might suppose were not discussed until modern scientific times. In *The City of God* (AD 426), Augustine of Hippo wrestled with the following questions, among others. Were the six days of creation described in Genesis 1 days such as we know them, or did the days stand for much longer periods? How was it that light was created three days before the creation of the sun and the moon? Before the Flood, we read in Genesis that people lived for hundreds of years, and that in some cases, they did not begin to have children until they were over one hundred and fifty years old. Are we to understand these years as the same as our years, or could they have been much shorter? Were there really giants on the earth in the days before the Flood?

Augustine answered as follows. The days and the light mentioned in Genesis 1 were different from what we understand by days and light. 'What kind of days these were it is extremely difficult, or perhaps impossible for us to conceive, and how much more to say!' (Book 11, ch. 6). On the lengths of the lives of those who lived before the Flood, Augustine had no doubt that their years were the same as our years. It was obvious that the years mentioned in the account of the Flood had ordinary days and months like our years, and there was no reason to suppose that the years of Genesis 5 were any different from those of Genesis 6—9. That some of them did not seem to have produced children until they were over one hundred and fifty was a difficulty. Either they did not have children until that age because they matured very much more slowly; or they deliberately abstained from having children. Augustine allowed that people before the Flood might have matured more slowly than people of his day, but his main solution to the problem was to suggest that they had produced more children than are mentioned in the Bible. If it was accepted that the children named in Genesis were only the important ones, and that they were not necessarily the firstborn, then the problem disappeared. The easiest problem to deal with was that of the giants. The tombs of ancient heroes showed them to have been of great stature, and Augustine could even give a recent example. Shortly before the fall of Rome (AD 410), there was a woman in that city who towered above all the people, even though her parents were not as tall as the tallest. In fact, visitors to Rome made a point of trying to catch a glimpse of this woman, so as to marvel at her stature. If this had been true recently, argued Augustine, it was not difficult to accept that in ancient times, there had been far more people on earth with such great height.

These explanations offered by Augustine may seem crude to us. But the methods used by him did not differ fundamentally from those used by critical scholars today. In the first place, he was aware of the problems raised by the text because the text appeared to contradict what was known about the world by observation and experience. In dealing with these problems, (a) he compared parts of the text with other parts, as in the demonstration that the years lived before the Flood were of the same length as during and after the Flood; (b) he suggested that the text might omit information, and not, therefore, be a complete record; (c) he appealed to secular evidence. By any standards, Augustine was a man of outstanding intellect, and if his work seems to us to be naive, this is only because the resources and expectations of his day were quite different from those of today. In spite of this cultural difference, we can see that parts of the Old Testament were as perplexing to intelligent people fifteen hundred years ago, as they were one hundred years ago.

The twelfth century saw the production of one of the greatest books on Old Testament interpretation ever written. Its author was the Jewish philosopher and physician Maimonides (1138–1204) who grew up in a part of Spain under Muslim rule, before moving to Egypt where he wrote *The Guide of the Perplexed* (*c.*1190). Muslim civilization had, from the eighth century, enjoyed a renaissance of science and philosophy, in which the philosophy of the fourth-century BC Greek philosopher Aristotle played an important part. In Muslim Spain, this philosophy was studied with great care, and it had a profound influence upon Maimonides. Whether Aristotle was correctly understood in Muslim Spain is not the issue here. Maimonides became convinced that Aristotle had correctly described the nature and functioning of the visible universe, and that he had rightly taught that God was incorporeal (without body or parts). Maimonides was impatient with religious apologists, including Christians, who began their speculations not with the world as it actually was, but with propositions derived from their imagination, and framed so as to reconcile reality with religious beliefs. 'I shall say to you that the matter is as Themistus puts it', he wrote. 'That which exists does not conform to the various opinions, but rather the correct opinions conform to that which exists' (*Guide*, I, ch. 71).

But could this approach, which accepted the primacy of philosophical and scientific accounts of reality, be reconciled with the Bible? Maimonides believed that it could, and in *The Guide of the Perplexed*, he argued that the prophets, and supremely Moses, were themselves philosophers with a highly developed faculty of imagination. For this reason, the divine law which they taught was the necessary guide for human conduct.

The Guide begins with an examination of biblical language, especially with the many 'human' terms which are used in connection with God: face, hand, image, went up, went down, etc. Whereas these terms might lead us to think that God has a body and parts, this is not the case, and the words cannot be taken at face value. God does not have a face or a hand, and he does not move. He does not even exist in the way that the world and its contents exist. There is also a discussion about prophecy and prophetic inspiration, based upon Aristotelian philosophical teaching about the constitution of man and his intellect. This discussion shows how it is necessary to interpret passages in which God is said to have 'spoken' to his servants. According to Maimonides, no divine communication takes place except through a vision of prophecy or a dream of prophecy. Some passages make this clear: 'The word of the LORD came to Abram in a vision' (Gen. 15.1). Where the vision is not mentioned in a biblical text, it must be assumed. 'It is known and established as a principle that no prophecy and no prophetic revelation come in any way except in a dream or in a vision and through the agency of an angel' (*Guide*, II, ch. 41). A further implication of this is that in 'miraculous' passages such as Genesis 18 where Abraham saw the three men who somehow represented God, Gen. 32.22ff. where Jacob wrestled with an angel, and Num. 22.22ff. where Balaam's she-ass spoke to her master, it was necessary to conclude that these were visions of prophecy, and not happenings that occurred in a normal state.

Some of the views expressed in *The Guide* were not new. Christian tradition had long ceased to take literally statements about God in human terms. Augustine (*City of God*, XI, 11) pointed out in regard to Genesis 6.6 that God could not repent, and that the phrase was a metaphor. Long after Maimonides, Calvin would make a similar point about this, and like passages. For Calvin, 'repented' refers to our understanding of God, but not to God as he really is. The greatness of *The Guide* lies in the way in which its author took with the utmost seriousness the world in which he lived, and the way in which that world was understood by science and philosophy. To say this does not, of course, commit us today to the sort of rationalizing solutions that Maimonides seems to have imposed upon the Bible. It shows us, however, that it is no new thing in biblical interpretation to accept that truth is one, that if the Bible has any significance for the world it has significance for the world as it is perceived intelligently, and that biblical interpretation is not simply a matter of reading the text literally.

Maimonides was faced with the problems mentioned above because, on the whole, he tried to face up to what the text appeared to say at its surface level. In much Christian exegesis up to the

Reformation, it was possible to avoid some of these problems because of the belief that the Bible had four levels of meaning: literal, doctrinal, mystical and ethical. In practice, this meant that the Old Testament was allegorized—something found already in the New Testament itself (see Galatians 4.21–30). However, there is no doubt that one of the attractions of the allegorical method was precisely that it enabled interpreters to look for hidden meanings, without having to grapple with the problems raised by the plain meaning of the text. At the Reformation, the allegorical method was largely rejected by the Protestant Churches.

B *From the Reformation to 1750*

The Reformation in Europe in the first part of the sixteenth century was closely connected with a revival in biblical studies in the fifteenth century. The invention of printing had made Greek and Hebrew Bibles more widely available, and there was a revival of Hebrew studies among Christian scholars. Luther (1483–1546) was a professor of biblical studies, and he devoted the major share of his teaching to the Old Testament. He believed that he was following in the footsteps of St Paul by using a biblical principle in order to determine what in the Old Testament was central, and what was not. The doctrine of justification by faith was based upon the fact that God is for us in Jesus Christ. Where, in the Old Testament, God is seen to be acting for his people, the gospel can be found; and there are anticipations in the Old Testament of the acceptance, by the nations, of the gospel on the basis of faith (e.g. Luther on Psalm 117). Already in Luther there are anticipations of modern critical positions about the authorship of books of the Bible, without any awareness that this could possibly involve unfaithfulness to the Bible. Luther held that while the Pentateuch was Mosaic, it was not necessarily all by Moses. Many of the prophetic books were not necessarily entirely written by the prophets whose name they bore.

Another great leader of the Reformation, Calvin, was a much more systematic commentator than Luther. He was less prepared than Luther to discriminate between what was central in the Old Testament and what was not. But we see that Calvin adopted positions that were more critical than some conservative positions adopted in the nineteenth or twentieth centuries. In dealing with the creation of the waters above the firmament, Calvin allowed that to common sense, it was incredible that there should be waters above the heaven. But it was not incredible if it was allowed that what was described was the creation of the world as it looked to the Israelites. 'He who would learn astronomy, and other recondite arts, let him go elsewhere . . . the waters here meant are such as the rude and unlearned may perceive' (Calvin on Genesis 1.6).

Calvin was using an interesting principle here. These verses did not describe the creation in such a way as to be consistent with any foreseeable scientific discoveries. They were *accommodated* to what the unlearned man saw when he looked around him; rain clouds in the sky, and the sun moving round the earth, for example. It may be legitimate to conclude from this that Calvin did not necessarily expect the Bible to provide scientific information about the nature of the universe.

In the aftermath of the Reformation, from the latter part of the sixteenth century and into the seventeenth century, there arose what has been called Protestant scholasticism. In defending themselves against the Roman Catholic Church, and against each other, the Protestant Churches developed rigid doctrinal positions, in which the Bible played the subordinate role of supplying proof texts in order to justify Lutheran or Calvinistic or other Protestant positions. Views of biblical inspiration were affirmed which at their most extreme reduced the biblical writers to little more than instruments through which God had dictated his words. As against the early Church, there was little or no interest in textual criticism. It would be unfair to suggest that during this period the Bible was a dead letter. This would be to belittle the great Puritan commentaries, to mention only one example. But it was during this period that there flourished an approach to the Bible of which modern conservatism is the heir. Before the Reformation, while no orthodox Christian doubted that the Bible was inspired, it was also agreed that the rule of faith of the Church was the foundation for its interpretation; and as has been shown, this did not prevent an active critical tradition. In post-Reformation Protestant orthodoxy, while the Bible served to provide proof texts in order to support particular doctrinal positions, it was also believed that this doctrinal position was fully consistent with the Bible, and that ultimately, the Bible alone was sufficient. Scripture provided the basis for the interpretation of Scripture; but not in the radical way that we find in

Luther. It would not be unfair to say that during this period, the critical attitude to the Old Testament was more restricted than it had ever been before in the history of the Church. It was more restricted than in the early Church, and certainly lacked the radicalism of the first flush of the Reformation.

Towards the close of the seventeenth century, the first steps that were to result in the modern critical approach to the Old Testament were taken in an unexpected quarter—the Roman Catholic Church. A French priest, Richard Simon, undertook to expose the errors of Protestants by attacking the foundation of their faith, namely, their belief in the sufficiency of the Bible alone. Two of his lines of attack concern us here. The first concerned the text of the Bible. He argued that in fact we could not be absolutely certain what the original text of the Bible contained, and that Protestants were thus on shaky ground in depending upon the Bible for their faith. They believed in an infallible book whose precise text was uncertain. In support of his arguments, Simon undertook much pioneering research into the history of the text and versions of the Bible. Second, he accused Protestants of confusing authority with authenticity.

Protestants, following traditional Jewish and Christian views about the authorship of books of the Bible, regarded the books as the work of known inspired individuals such as Moses, Joshua, Samuel, David and Solomon. The authority of the Bible was supported by authenticity, that is, the belief that the books had been written by named, inspired individuals. Simon attacked this position by questioning the authenticity, or rather, the traditional views of the authorship of some books. He suggested that much composition had been done by scribal schools, that Moses was not the author of the entire Pentateuch, and that books such as Judges, Samuel and Kings had reached their present form long after the events described. Simon believed that provided a Roman Catholic scholar did not contradict the doctrines of the Church, he should be free to investigate such matters as the authorship of the books, and the history of the text of the Bible, in a critical manner. He was too far ahead of his time. His own Church, without ever formally condemning him, frustrated the distribution of his publications. Yet it was not able to prevent his influence entirely, as will be seen later.

Another important movement of the late seventeenth and early eighteenth centuries was Deism, which had its home in England. This was a philosophical form of religion which accepted reason as a sufficient guiding principle. It was obvious to reason that God had created the world, that the soul survived death, and that there were rewards for the righteous and punishments for the wicked. Deism was hostile to superstition, of which it found not a little in the Old Testament; and although Deism never directly challenged the authority of the Old Testament, it went a long way to undermining it.

Meanwhile, in the eighteenth century, English Deism spread to Germany, where it played a major part in the renewal of German critical scholarship. One of the fathers of the modern critical method in Germany was J. S. Semler. He had been brought up in pietist circles, in a type of Protestantism which laid great stress upon personal experience, especially experience of conversion, and which had been represented in Britain by the Methodist revival of the eighteenth century. In addition to his pietist background, Semler was familiar with English Deist writings, as well as with the work of Richard Simon, which he arranged to have translated into German. Semler was also deeply interested in Luther, whom he studied on the basis of manuscript evidence as well as the semi-reliable printed editions of Luther's works.

Richard Simon had found in the teaching authority of the Church the firm foundation on the basis of which he could conduct his critical investigations of the Bible. Semler found his firm foundation in the doctrine of justification by faith. The primary purpose of Scripture was to speak to the individual the word of assurance by which he knew that God had reconciled him to himself in Jesus Christ. Granted this assurance, the Christian scholar had the liberty to investigate the Bible freely and fearlessly. Semler used the principle of justification as a criterion for defining what was central in the Old Testament. Where the Old Testament described the work of God in vindicating his people, there was the gospel. Other material was less important. With the work of Semler, the era of the modern historical critical study of the Old Testament can be said to have begun.

C   *The new element in critical study from 1750*

Was critical study of the Old Testament fundamentally different after roughly 1750 from what it was previously? If so, what has been the point in this essay of trying to show that, in one sense, Old Testament study has always been critical? With regard to the methods of critical scholarship after 1750 compared with before that date, there was no fundamental difference. In both periods, scholars were concerned with textual criticism and with the study of the biblical languages. In both, what was known about the history, customs and physical geography of the land of the Bible was collected and studied. In both, scholars tried to face up to the problems raised by apparent contradictions between the Bible and philosophical and scientific accounts of the world. What was new after 1750 was that critical investigation had an open-endedness that it did not possess before. Before 1750, even the most radical investigations in mainstream Christianity or Judaism were bound ultimately to stay within certain bounds. Maimonides accepted, and devoutly believed in, the superiority of Moses and in the divine origin of the Mosaic law. Simon was a devout Roman Catholic who did not doubt the teaching authority of his Church. It would be wrong to suggest that after 1750 scholars ceased to be devout, and that the openness of their method inevitably led to scepticism and heresy, although this was the charge commonly brought against critical scholars in the nineteenth century. If a critical scholar believed, with Semler, that the Bible spoke words of assurance of reconciliation to God through Jesus Christ, it is difficult to see how this could lead to scepticism, unless Christianity was defined in such a way as to commit all believers to particular views about who had written the books of the Bible. And it was not only in the circles of critical scholarship that 'heresy' could arise. Orthodox Protestantism in the seventeenth and eighteenth centuries produced 'Unitarianism' among those who so upheld the sufficiency of the Bible, that they rejected any sort of assent to the doctrine of the Trinity as defined in the early Church, and reaffirmed at the Reformation, because the Bible did not require such assent from believers.

On the other hand, it must be accepted that once it was conceded that the Bible could be studied 'like any other book', it was in theory possible for scholars to reach conclusions at variance with

Christianity. Of course, long before 1750, the study of the Bible had led some people to views which were against the prevailing orthodoxy, with the result that they left, or were excluded from, their churches. After 1750, it was easier in some churches for those with unorthodox views to remain in membership. The difference between the situation before 1750 and after, can, perhaps, be summed up as follows. Before 1750, critical scholarship was ultimately a defence of whatever type of orthodoxy a scholar accepted, for all that he might well make far-reaching concessions to contemporary philosophic or scientific views. After 1750, critical scholars were more prepared to let their biblical scholarship challenge their own orthodoxy. Their scholarship was far more of an open-ended quest for truth, than a quest for truth limited by acceptance of an orthodoxy, whether that orthodoxy was concerned with the verbal inspiration of Scripture, or the teaching authority of the Roman Catholic Church.

It is at this point that it may be correct to identify the difficulty which new students experience. The use which is made of the Bible in churches is very properly a use directed towards specific evangelistic, doctrinal and theological ends. Any preacher worth his salt does not spend his time in the pulpit pointing out difficulties which the Bible contains. He makes a positive proclamation. On the other hand, ordinary worshippers are aware that the Bible is not a simple book to understand, and that it appears to be in conflict with modern scientific accounts of the world. In some cases, churches may help worshippers to tackle these critical questions through study groups. In other cases, there may be no occasion where worshippers can discuss their difficulties openly, and they may either conclude for themselves, or be told straight out, that it is un-Christian to entertain the idea that critical questions can be addressed to the Bible. But one of the points of the first part of this historical sketch of biblical criticism has been to show that it is quite false to equate a questioning and critical attitude with unfaithfulness to the Bible. It cannot be maintained that it is wrong to ask critical questions, and wrong to use reason and the intellect to try to solve critical problems. If we accept this, then we condemn Augustine, Luther, Calvin and many others. Nevertheless, it appears to be true that, because many beginners in biblical studies do not have, nor can be expected to have, any knowledge of the history of critical study, they are upset or put off even by the sort of critical approaches that existed before 1750, in the so-called pre-critical period.

At the end of this essay, some of the points made in this section will be mentioned again. It now remains to sketch the development of the critical method from 1750.

D *From 1750*

If the rise of modern critical Old Testament study meant that scholars no longer tied themselves to conclusions dictated by doctrinal beliefs, but were prepared to follow wherever the truth seemed to lead them, this does not mean that scholarship became unbiased. On the contrary, critical scholarship was now exposed to the danger that assumptions taken from philosophy would occupy the place vacated by doctrinal beliefs. This was all the more dangerous when this process went unnoticed, and critical scholars believed that they really were unbiased. This is why critical scholarship, if it is to remain truly critical, must always be aware of its basic assumptions, and must be subjecting these to critical scrutiny. To give one example, British Old Testament scholars in the last decades of the nineteenth century accepted that religion, like morality and society, had developed from 'lower' to 'higher' forms. This was the common view of the time, and it led scholars to interpret the Old Testament in a developmentalist way, although the Old Testament itself provides little, if any, evidence for the view that Israel's religion 'improved' as time went on. In the present century, different, and one hopes more adequate, understandings of the nature of religion have enabled the nineteenth-century opinions to be critically reviewed.

As we have seen, it is a German scholar, J. S. Semler, who has come to be regarded as the father of modern critical Old Testament scholarship. It was in Germany that the method became increasingly influential until, in about 1860, it was dominant. To say this is not in any way to decry the work of the scholars in Germany of great learning and critical acumen in the pre-1750 sense. In Britain, the progress of the new critical method was much slower. The decline of Deism after 1750, and the rise of pietistic forms of Christianity in the Methodist Church and parts of the Church of England made the conditions for the acceptance of the critical method largely unfavourable. Yet it is surprising to discover how liberal British Old Testament scholars were in some ways in the period 1750–1860. During this period, many alterations to the Hebrew text were suggested which in some cases rested upon nothing more than intelligent guesswork. Indeed, many of the emendations familiar in modern Old Testament study were first suggested at this time. It was also allowed that prophetic books had been subject to editorial presentation, and that not everything in a prophetic book was to be regarded as the work of the prophet himself. Even William Paley, in his celebrated *Evidences of Christianity* (1794) argued that it was quite mistaken to make the truth of Christianity depend upon 'the circumstantial truth of each separate passage of the Old Testament, the genuineness of every book, the information, fidelity, and judgement of every writer in it' (*Evidences*, Part III, ch. 3).

In Germany, particular attention was paid to three overlapping areas of study: the sources of the Pentateuch, the history of Israel, and the development of Israelite religion. As early as 1753 it had been suggested that Moses had used two different sources in the composition of Genesis chapters 1 and 2, in view of the different divine names used consistently in those chapters. This suggestion provided the impetus for the attempt to detect different documents or sources throughout the whole of the Pentateuch.

The isolation of sources led to a new approach to the history of Israel. Previously, the historical parts of the Old Testament had been interpreted as a collection of true stories containing moral and religious instruction. But in 1812, Barthold Georg Niebuhr began to publish his history of Rome, indicating in the process that it was possible to reconstruct history scientifically with the aid of a careful and critical evaluation of sources. What Niebuhr had done for Rome, Heinrich Ewald began to do for ancient Israel from 1843 onwards. Needless to say, a history of Israel based upon a critical evaluation of the source material in the Old Testament was bound to come into conflict with the story as presented in the Old Testament—a problem which is discussed fully in the next chapter.

The study of Israelite religion was strongly influenced by philosophical theories about the nature of religion that were current in Germany between 1800 and 1850. Of particular importance was a view that distinguished between the spontaneous religion of a people in its 'infancy', and a cultic, priestly, doctrinal form of religion into which the spontaneous form developed. In the late

1870s, Julius Wellhausen achieved a brilliant synthesis of the researches that had been going on in the three areas mentioned. He presented a version of the history of Israelite religion which distinguished three phases, each phase corresponding to a document or documents that made up the Pentateuch. The documents J and E (ninth–eighth centuries BC) were evidence for a spontaneous early phase in Israel's religion, before the onset of the second phase in which there was concern for the centralization of worship and cultic regulation, as reflected in the D document (much of the book Deuteronomy). After the Exile, Israelite religion was completely dominated by the priests and by the minutiae of cultic regulation, as seen in the Priestly document (now embedded in Genesis–Numbers, but especially in Leviticus). Much of the material traditionally ascribed to Moses, for example, the institution of the priesthood and the sacrificial system, was, according to this approach, no earlier than the sixth century BC. Critical scholarship with its open-endedness had produced a description of the history of Israelite religion radically at variance with that in the Old Testament itself. To take the history of Old Testament beyond Wellhausen up to present times would be illuminating, but would only reproduce the excellent work of R. E. Clements, whose book, *A Century of Old Testament Study* (Guildford 1976) is recommended for further reading.

In Britain, the critical method was imported from Germany during the first part of the nineteenth century, but it made slow progress. The Catholic renewal in the Church of England from the mid-1830s commonly known as the Oxford Movement saw in biblical criticism an attack on the doctrine of the divinity of Jesus. If statements by Jesus in the New Testament about the authorship of Old Testament books were contradicted by biblical criticism, this implied that Jesus could be wrong on spiritual matters (if matters of authorship were spiritual matters) and his divinity was called into question. For example, in Matthew 19.8, Jesus ascribes the law about divorce in Deuteronomy 24.1–4 to Moses, whereas as early as 1804, a critical scholar had argued that Deuteronomy was written long after the time of Moses. Thus, for the high church party, the fight against critical Old Testament scholarship was the front line in the defence of the divinity of Jesus. However, it should be pointed out that orthodox belief in the divinity of Jesus does not necessarily demand his infallibility in matters of human fact.

It was not only in high church Anglican circles that biblical criticism was regarded with suspicion. In 1857, Samuel Davidson was dismissed from his chair of Old Testament at the Lancashire Independent College, for writing an *Introduction to the Old Testament* that followed some of the German critical views. Davidson himself passionately affirmed his evangelical beliefs, and maintained that critical scholarship was not incompatible with those beliefs. In 1860, the publication of a set of essays by members of the 'broad' church party in the Church of England, entitled *Essays and Reviews*, resulted in the trial of two of the essayists because of their (mildly) critical views.

For over fifty years, the Regius chair of Hebrew at Oxford was occupied by E. B. Pusey, one of the leaders of the Oxford Movement. His aversion to German critical scholarship was based upon a knowledge of German (something rather exceptional when he was appointed to his professorship in 1828) and upon contact with both critical and more conservative scholars in Germany. When he died in 1882, to be succeeded the following year by S. R. Driver, one epoch ended and another began.[2] When he was appointed, Driver was known primarily as an expert in the Hebrew language. He soon set about showing how, in his opinion, the new scientific learning and biblical criticism could be accepted without rejecting the theological value of the Old Testament. He achieved this by regarding as the centre of the Old Testament the teaching of the prophets on ethical monotheism and social justice. The Old Testament witnessed to a process of moral and religious development, in which process the educating hand of God was to be discerned. Driver's two most important works, his *Introduction to the Literature of the Old Testament*, and his commentary on the book of Genesis, went into many editions, and were responsible for helping many thoughtful people to see that the results of critical scholarship were compatible with deeply held Christian convictions. It has been said of the Genesis commentary that it saved the faith of a generation of thinkers who could not deny the correctness of the post-Darwinian account of the world, and who did not see how this could be reconciled with a literal reading of Genesis. From the time of Driver's appointment, the critical method made steady progress in Britain, although it has always tended to be more cautious, and less given to far-reaching theories, than in Germany.

In the United States of America, the critical method became established early in the nineteenth century, backed by translations of critical works from Germany. A leading scholar was Moses Stuart (1780–1852), who was professor at Andover Seminary, Massachusetts, from 1812, and who is said to have had a greater command of critical German literature than any other American of his day. There was a small but steady flow of Americans who went to Germany in order to complete their studies.

However, the introduction of the critical method in the United States did not escape opposition. The second half of the nineteenth century saw the rise of dispensational pre-millennarianism, which developed the old idea that God was dealing with mankind through successive covenants, or dispensations. Dispensationalism was a sophisticated method of biblical interpretation which partitioned biblical history into distinct phases. Some of these phases were relevant only to God's plans for the Jews, and they had no direct application to the Church apart from being evidence for divine activity. Dispensationalism totally rejected all forms of historical or literary criticism as applied to the Bible. Towards the end of the nineteenth century, controversy within the Presbyterian Church of America about the inspiration of the Bible led to the trials for heresy of two prominent OT scholars, Charles A. Briggs of Union Seminary, New York (1893), and Henry Preserved Smith of Lane Seminary, Cincinnati (1894). Both were later contributors to the outstanding Anglo-American *International Critical Commentary*. Briggs had studied in Berlin with Emil Rödiger, and had a deep knowledge of German critical scholarship.

E   *Modern conservatism and biblical criticism*

The academic and critical study of the Bible in Britain is largely undertaken in departments in secular universities. (The situation in the United States is, of course, rather more complex.) In many cases, universities have statutes which prohibit denominational religious teaching. In such university departments, the teaching is based upon research, which is itself based upon the fundamental tenet of the critical method, namely, that scholars are free to follow in their work what they sincerely believe to be the truth, even if that begins to question the religious and academic assumptions that they hold. The content of the syllabuses is to some degree determined by what happen to be the central issues in scholarship at the time (see the opening of this chapter). Universities are not the only places where the Bible is studied. There are theological colleges or seminaries, and Bible and missionary training colleges. In these, the OT may well be studied critically, but usually within the limits of the specific aims of these colleges. It is no part of this essay to suggest that what these institutions do is wrong, or unacademic

Students who come to study the Bible at university enter an academic discipline as rigorous as any. They are required to be something of a linguist, a historian, and a person with literary and artistic appreciation. Students who come from conservative backgrounds may suffer from an initial shock. They may come from a type of Christianity that is descended from the later phase of the Reformation in the late sixteenth and seventeenth centuries. As has been seen above, this phase was a good deal less critical than the scholarship that was found in the early Church and the beginning of the Reformation.

Whatever beliefs students may bring with them when they begin their academic studies, it is not right for university departments to try to destroy those beliefs, and to substitute for them the opinions of the teachers. This would amount to an infringement of the intellectual integrity of a student. Students must rather be presented with the evidence, the resources for tackling questions, and some guidance about elementary logic, so that they may reach their own conclusions.

There is one question which the present writer puts constantly to his more conservative students, and which can serve to end this chapter. The Bible says of itself that it is inspired by God (2 Timothy 3.16). Does this statement necessarily mean that only traditional views of the authorship of books of the Bible can be correct? Does it necessarily exclude the possibility that books had more than one writer, and that literary sources were used? On what grounds is it permissible to limit the power of God by saying that although he could have inspired one writer of a biblical book, he could not possibly have inspired several authors or redactors? Critical views of the origin and growth of the Bible do not, as is often suggested, undermine belief in the inspiration and authority of the Bible, even if they may demand different ways of using the Bible as compared with 'literal' or 'dispensational' ways of reading it

Critical views, by showing the complexity and indeed the 'ordinariness' of the growth of the Bible, require a deep and sophisticated view of the divine guiding as a result of which the Bible is *not* like any other book, even when it is studied critically like any other book.

NOTES

1 See the margin to the Revised Version and the American Standard Version of 1 Samuel 13.1.

2 Later Anglo-Catholics were more open than Pusey to critical scholarship; e.g., Charles Gore, ed., *Lux Mundi* (London, John Murray, 1889), and especially C. A. Simpson, Regius Professor of Hebrew, afterward Dean of Christ Church, who in *The Early Traditions of Israel* (Oxford, Blackwell, 1948) pressed source criticism to distant limits.

FOR FURTHER READING

Brief summaries of the history of Old Testament interpretation can be found in *The Interpreter's Dictionary of the Bible*, 4 vols. & supp. (London, SCM, 1977; Nashville, Abingdon, 1976) and in the following works:

T. K. Cheyne, *Founders of Old Testament Criticism* (London, 1893; Jerusalem, Raritas, 1971);

R. E. Clements, *A Century of Old Testament Study* (Guildford, Lutterworth, 1976);

—*One Hundred Years of Old Testament Interpretation* (Philadelphia, Westminster, 1976);

E. G. Kraeling, *The Old Testament since the Reformation* (London, Lutterworth, 1955; New York, Harper & Row, 1955).

For a specialist treatment of the origins of biblical criticism in the United States see J. W. Brown, *The Rise of Biblical Criticism in America, 1800–1870* (Middletown, Wesleyan University, 1969). For a Roman Catholic view see Jean Levie, *The Bible, Word of God in Words of Men* (London, Geoffrey Chapman, 1961; New York, P. J. Kenedy, 1962). For a detailed discussion of Fundamentalism, see J. Barr, *Fundamentalism* (London, SCM, 1977; Philadelphia, Westminster, 1978).

2

Methods in Old Testament Study

DAVID J. A. CLINES

Methods are a means to an end; so before we speak of methods in OT study, we must speak of *goals* in OT study. Many, perhaps most, people come to the study of the Bible with religious goals in mind: they want to know more about the Bible because they believe it will deepen their faith, communicate God's will to them, and so on. They have a preconception about the nature of the Bible as the word of God, the final authority in matters of faith and practice, or as the deposit of the religious experiences of ancient Jews and Christians, a valuable resource book for religious believers of today. They would therefore be inclined to agree with the dictum of the Danish philosopher Søren Kierkegaard, 'God's word is given in order that thou shalt act in accordance with it, not in order that thou shalt practise the art of interpreting obscure passages'[1]—even if they might not put it in quite his words. Nevertheless, biblical study is—to some extent—a matter of practising the art of interpreting obscure passages, and those who have religious goals as their aim need to realize that biblical study of itself will not reach those goals, though it would be surprising if it did not have a great deal of religious pay-off (to put it crudely). The academic study of the Bible has been, and must be, one in which people of any religious faith, or of none, can engage, and can co-operate. The immediate goal of biblical study must be one that allows but does not require religious preconceptions; for many, the immediate goal may be only a stage on the way to an ultimate (religious) goal, but for others it may be a sufficient goal in itself.

Let us suggest that the primary goal in biblical study should be *understanding*. Other goals people have in studying the OT, like learning Hebrew, or discovering the facts about the history of Israel or passing examinations, even ultimate goals like deepening one's religious faith, can best be regarded as secondary goals in the *academic* study of the Old Testament. For only some goal like

26

'understanding' accords both with the nature of the subject matter and with the nature of academic study. Given that there is an Old Testament (or, Hebrew Bible), what else can be done about it in an institution of higher education? It cannot be preached, and it cannot be 'taught'—as doctrine, that is, as what one ought to believe; for a university or college is not the place for that. But neither can it be used simply as a textbook for ancient history or as a source for illustrating social customs in the ancient Near East; for it was self-evidently not for these purposes that the Hebrew Bible was brought together in the form that it has and it does not as a whole have the character of a history or a manual of social customs. Only some description like 'the Scriptures of the Hebrew people', or 'the sacred writings of the Jews which now form part of the Christian Bible', can do justice to its essence. It is a religious document, and the most appropriate way of handling a religious document in an academic setting is to attempt to *understand* it.

When we come to formulate our understanding, of part or whole of the Old Testament, we call that formulation or putting into words an *interpretation*. And since it is probably impossible to understand without putting into words, at least in one's own mind, one might as well say perhaps that 'interpretation' should be the chief aim of Old Testament study. I prefer, however, to say 'understanding', since that focuses on the processes by which one comes to understand, rather than 'interpretation', which focuses on the crystallization of that understanding. Nevertheless, using the term 'interpretation' is a useful reminder of what kind of writing about the OT is most appropriate to its nature. Those works which illuminate the text by offering an interpretation, whether of a phrase or a book, the meaning of a verse or the structure of a biblical author's thought, are the most suited to its character. While not all commentaries are illuminating, the commentary form is the quintessential mode of biblical interpretation; but the essay on character, plot, or theology can be equally valuable for the interpretation of larger passages.

One other term, frequently encountered in biblical studies, needs to be introduced at this point, namely *exegesis*. 'Exegesis' is nothing but interpretation, but the term is usually reserved for the kind of interpretation that explains phrase by phrase or verse by verse the biblical passage; 'interpretation' may refer to a more discursive treatment of longer stretches of biblical text.

If we allow now that the primary goal of Old Testament study is *understanding*, which is expressed in interpretation, either large-scale or more narrowly exegetical, we may go on to ask what methods are appropriate for gaining understanding. I would distinguish between first-order methods, which have understanding as their chief intention, and second-order methods, which are not principally intended to interpret the biblical text, but which nevertheless often have some valuable contribution to make to interpretation.

A   *First-order methods*

Biblical interpretation has been going on for a long time (see chapter 1), ever since any part of the Bible was composed, in fact, for every hearer or reader is an interpreter of what he hears or reads—otherwise he does not understand what he hears or reads. Certain methods that have been successful in biblical interpretation have acquired names familiar to biblical scholars—though unfamiliar to many experts in the interpretation of other literary texts, even religious texts. I will discuss first three of these methods traditional in biblical scholarship, and then three other methods more familiar to students of other literatures. None of the methods discussed in this chapter is wholly distinct from other methods; some have fairly clear procedures, while others are more an approach or an attitude to the text; there is no predetermined sequence in which these methods can most fruitfully be applied, and no way of telling in advance which will yield the best results; and in many cases one is not aware of using a particular method.

1   *Traditional methods in biblical scholarship*

a. Historical-grammatical exegesis.   This is in fact not so much *a* method, but more a way of life to most biblical scholars. It refers to the endeavour to interpret any passage according to the natural sense of the words ('grammatical') and according to the probable meaning of the author in his own time ('historical'). As a method, it functions first as a warning against arbitrary or fanciful interpretations, such as were often (but not invariably) to be encountered in pre-Reformation interpretation. Thus, while an allegorical interpretation of the OT often saw in the name Jerusalem a veiled reference to the pious Christian soul or to the heavenly city, the historical-*grammatical* method insists that 'Jerusalem' in the OT always refers to the ancient city of that name, unless there is good evidence to the contrary. Or, whereas the commentary on the prophecy of Habakkuk composed by members of the Dead Sea scrolls community at Qumran apparently interpreted the 'righteous' and 'wicked' referred to by Habakkuk (in the late seventh century BC) as persons contemporary with the Qumran community, in the first century BC, the *historical-*grammatical method insists that these words should refer to those persons intended by the prophet. (In this case, it is clear that Hab. 1.4 refers to 'righteous' and 'wicked' men of Habakkuk's own time.)

Such an approach may seem obvious enough to us, but we may note that it may lead to apparent *loss* of understanding rather than gain. Thus, the statement of God in Gen. 1.26, 'Let us make man in our image', was readily interpreted by the church fathers as an address by God the Father to the other persons of the Trinity. As exegetes of the historical-grammatical school, we would have to deny that the author of Genesis 1 knew anything of the doctrine of the Trinity, and to deny therefore that such can be the meaning; but, though many suggestions have been made, no entirely convincing interpretation of the plural ('us', 'our') can be offered. In such cases, we can only plead that to understand *less* is not necessarily to understand *worse*. Again, the historical-grammatical method can *create* problems which do not exist if its rigours are not applied. So references in the Psalms to the king, especially to the king as God's son (Ps. 2.7), were traditionally interpreted by Christian scholars as references to the Messiah, Christ. If the historical-grammatical method is followed, however, the king must be seen as the contemporary Israelite king, and some explanation must be found for references to him as God's son and for the address to him as 'God' (Ps. 45.6—if that is what the Hebrew actually says).

Despite such problems, the historical-grammatical approach is universally accepted, principally because it offers a criterion for judging between rival interpretations. It is not so clear to all scholars today, however, as it was even a few decades ago, that the meaning of a passage should be restricted to 'the meaning intended by the author'. This doubt arises partly because authors (especially poets) do not always intend one meaning and one meaning only, and partly because re-applications of a prophet's words (for example) to later situations—a process which was going on already in the OT period and which is clearly evident in the New Testament—can be argued to draw out fresh, legitimate, meanings from those words which the prophet himself never intended. This is a debate that has barely started in earnest; but it is doubtful whether the historical-grammatical approach can ever now be dispensed with, and the (presumed) meanings intended by the author will always be an important constituent, if not the sum total, of the meaning and hence the interpretation of a passage.

b. Textual criticism. Historical-grammatical exegesis interprets the texts; but what is the text? Obviously we do not have the original manuscripts of any biblical book. The oldest Hebrew manuscripts come from the second century BC, but they are mostly fragmentary; the oldest datable complete Hebrew Bible is from the eleventh century AD. While all the evidence shows that on the whole the original texts of the biblical writings have been copied faithfully down through the centuries, in the exact wording there are thousands of variations. It is impossible to know with complete precision what the books of Amos or Job, for example, originally said; but it is possible to reconstruct a better (i.e. more likely to be original) text than exists in any surviving manuscript.

The discipline that strives to reach behind the medieval manuscripts to the probable precise wording of the biblical books is known as textual criticism. In many respects it is a rigorously objective discipline, with elaborate rules for the evaluation of any piece of textual evidence. From another point of view, however, it is a form of interpretation, since the ultimate arbiter of any textual evidence is the scholar's (or scholars') judgement about its intelligibility. So the fact that all the manuscripts and the ancient versions (in some cases centuries older than our Hebrew manuscripts) agree on the wording of a verse does not necessarily mean that the verse makes sense or that it reproduces what the author originally wrote. In Amos 6.12, for example, the Hebrew and the versions have 'Does one plough with oxen?' in a sequence of rhetorical questions that are meant to be answered 'No!' An emendation (i.e. proposed correction) of the Hebrew yields the sense 'Does one plough the sea with oxen?' which is just the absurd kind of question required by the context; RSV, NEB and most modern versions translate accordingly, convinced that this is more probably what Amos said. (What is involved is dividing one Hebrew word into two and supplying different vowels, *bbqr ym*, pronounced *babbāqār yām*, instead of *bbqrym*, pronounced *babbᵉqārim*.) Another situation arises when the ancient versions agree in differing from the Hebrew text. A well-known example occurs in Gen. 4.8, where the Hebrew manuscripts have 'Cain said to Abel his brother' but do not tell us what he said (the Hebrew verb does mean 'said' rather than 'spoke'). The Samaritan text of the Pentateuch, the Greek Septuagint, the Latin Vulgate, and two of the three Aramaic Targums (paraphrasing translations) have something like 'Let us go into the fields'. Here the only rule a textual critic can offer by way of advice is not very helpful: he will say that the Samaritan and the Greek when agreeing against the Hebrew of Genesis are not necessarily preferable. So in the end the scholar must decide whether he thinks the ancient versions have preserved a phrase accidentally omitted from the Hebrew, or whether the ancient versions have made an addition to the Hebrew because they were as puzzled by the Hebrew as we are. The RSV inserts the addition, explaining in a footnote that the addition is based on the versions, while the NEB inserts it without explaining that it is an addition; the RV fudged the issue by translating 'Cain *told* Abel his brother'.

It is often thought that textual criticism provides a foundation upon which exegesis builds; the examples above show that while most of the business of textual criticism (collecting evidence, generalizing about the tendencies of a version or the relationship of manuscripts) is not exegesis and could be regarded as preparatory to it, the point of decision in a matter of textual criticism belongs to the work of interpretation. Establishing the text and interpreting the text are enterprises that go hand in hand.

c. Redaction criticism. A 'redactor' is the jargon of biblical studies for what is elsewhere called an 'editor'. The term comes from the stage in biblical criticism when the authors of biblical books (e.g. the Gospels) were regarded as essentially compilers or editors of sources rather than as authors in their own right. But today, when authors of biblical books are increasingly seen as more than merely editors, the rather misleading term 'redaction criticism' is still applied to the search for the distinctive viewpoint, or intention, of the author that is expressed in the shape and organization of his work, its contents, its principle of selection and omission, as well as in express statements of intention by the author. English-speaking scholars have not adopted the German term sometimes used for such study, *Tendenz* or 'tendency' criticism, though this is a more appropriate term.

An example of where 'redaction' or 'tendency' criticism can be applied to good effect is the history work running from Joshua to 2 Kings, known as the 'Deuteronomistic History' because the style and outlook of the author have much in common with the book of Deuteronomy. A careful reader of this history will not imagine that it was written simply to record the past, but will find in it clues to the author's intention, purpose, or bias. Some of the evidence is explicit, as in his famous judgements upon the kings of Israel and Judah that they 'did evil [or occasionally, 'good'] in the eyes of the LORD'. Some of the evidence is implicit, as in the fact that he included many narratives of prophetic figures (e.g. Elijah and Elisha) and that he began his work with Joshua and the judges and ended it with the fall of Jerusalem. Putting all the evidence together, we may say that the author's purpose was to establish that the monarchy was an institution fatal for Israel, or that the destruction of Israel and Judah came about because they gave too little heed to the prophets or because the worship of foreign gods was tolerated in Israel—or some more subtle blending of such statements. However we define the intention or 'tendency' of the work, by doing so we are fashioning a major interpretative tool for the understanding of the whole work and each of its parts.

Redaction criticism in the strictest sense is a study of how the author used his sources. In the case of the Deuteronomistic History, the sources are mostly hypothetical, though it is entirely reasonable to suppose that some parts were drawn from royal annals, some from a collection of stories, whether written or oral, about heroes ('judges'), some from a series of tales about prophets. If the sources can be reconstructed with any degree of certainty and if the author's own shaping of them (addition, deletion, compression, etc.) can be detected, we have further evidence to put toward our comprehensive picture of his 'tendency'. In the study of the Gospels, if we can be sure that Matthew used Mark as a written source, redaction criticism can be very finely tuned to take into account minute deviations by the author from his source. But more often than not, the same results can be obtained by focusing upon the work itself and upon the interrelationship of its parts.

Redaction criticism, however it is understood, is an aspect of the historical-grammatical approach, and not really another method to be ranked alongside it. Its concern, however, is more with the meaning of the writing as a whole than with the small parts that exegesis is devoted to. And its prominence in recent decades is symptomatic of current interest in larger wholes rather than verse-by-verse details; but both the wholes and the parts have to be studied in careful balance.

2 Methods in literary criticism

a. Close reading. The practice of 'close reading' is sometimes deplored because of its association with the New Criticism school of critics of English literature and because of the extravagance of some of its practitioners. But critics of every school implicitly or explicitly engage in something very like 'close reading', i.e. a careful and minute scrutiny of all aspects of the text's language, style, metaphors, images and their relation to one another. It is not a 'murdering to dissect'; in analysing the words on the page 'what we are doing is to bring into sharp focus, in turn, this, that and the other detail, juncture or relation in our total response . . . to dwell with a deliberate, considering responsiveness on this, that or the other node or focal point in the complete organization that the poem [or, 'literary work'] is.'[2]

Not unexpectedly, poetry is a more immediately rewarding subject for close reading than is prose. A biblical example that lends itself well to close reading is Hosea's fine poem about Yahweh and his adulterous wife Israel (Hos. 2.2–23). If we concentrate upon the primary image of the poem, that of the relationship, we sense the dominance of indicators of *belonging*: *my* wife, *her* husband, *her* children, *their* mother, *my* lovers, *my* wool, *my* flax, *my* oil, *my* drink, and many other such phrases. If we see that this is a poem about *belonging*, we have not tamed it or pigeonholed it, but we have sharpened our perception of it. We can go on to consider what kinds of belonging exist in the poem: there is *right* belonging ('my husband', v. 16), and *negation* of belonging ('not my wife', v. 2) and *wrong* belonging ('my lovers', v. 5). The whole poem, it turns out, explores this triple possibility in belonging. The acts of movement (coming, going, returning), of gift (giving, withholding, taking), of thought (remembering, forgetting, remembering wrongly), and of speech (responding, not responding, responding wrongly) are all developments of the fundamental three-way division in the primary image. The more these connections and resemblances are dwelt on and savoured, the more the poem manifests its unity of conception, and the deeper, consequently, the reader's understanding of it.

Close reading of a passage (a poem perhaps or a whole book), while it requires wholehearted concentration upon that text, does not demand that all other texts should be expunged from one's mind (if that were possible!), though some critics of 'close reading' have supposed that it does. For obviously one's general knowledge of life and particular knowledge of other works of the same author, or in the case of the OT, other OT books, contribute—often unconsciously—to one's understanding of a passage; the commentaries draw explicit attention to all kinds of such extraneous data. There is another type of extraneous knowledge, however, that can be very valuable even though it may be knowledge of what may not exist (!). That is to say, every text has a countertext, or rather, many countertexts, things that could have been said but weren't. What is actually spoken or written is always selected, consciously or not, from the countless possibilities inherent in the language known to the speaker or writer. Every sentence spoken or written has unexpressed and rejected counterparts lurking in the background. By conjuring up some of these countertexts, the reality, individuality, and lack of inevitability of the text before us can be reinforced. We call up such a countertext when we read in Isa. 53.2 that the servant of Yahweh 'grew up before him like a young plant, like a plant rooted in *dry* ground', and remark that the last phrase is hardly what we would expect; for the righteous are generally not weedy and underdeveloped, and if they are like plants, they are like plants by streams of water whose leaf does not wither (Ps. 1.3). To the servant of Yahweh is attributed a history contrary to expectation (hence the astonishment of onlookers, 52.15), and the countertext, which in this case exists in the background and which we are at least vaguely aware of, focuses our attention on something peculiar and unique about Isaiah 53 and so enriches our understanding.

b. The idea of the 'literary work of art'.   Whatever else the OT is, it is beyond question a literary work. There are some parts of it,

indeed, which could hardly be called 'literature' (e.g. the genealogies at the beginning of 1 Chronicles), except perhaps on a
minimalist definition of literature as 'what is written'. But the great
majority is literature—chiefly of the types story and poem—of
varying degrees of quality. The best suited approaches in studying
it are therefore not surprisingly those which are effective in
literature studies more generally. One such approach is the stress in
literature studies of the last half-century especially on the idea of the
'literary work of art'. This phrase stands for two distinct emphases:
(i) that the literary work should be primarily considered as a whole;
(ii) that the literary work should be studied for what it is in itself,
with relatively minor concentration on the historical circumstances
of its composition.

(i) The first emphasis is one that has emerged independently in
biblical studies in the development of redaction criticism (see
above). In literary criticism, it balances the stress on close reading,
which without the constraint of the total view can easily lead (and
has done so, with disastrous results) to atomistic interpretation,
frantic games of hunt-the-symbol, and arbitrary interpretations
that astound the reader with how much can be got out of, or read
into, a line like George Herbert's 'Man stole the fruit, but I must
climb the tree' (Christ is a Prometheus figure, the climbing is a
Jack-on-the-Beanstalk myth, the son stealing from his father's
orchard is an incest symbol, according to William Empson).[3] The
holistic, total view, while always open to revision in the light of the
merest detail, must have the last word in interpretation. In the quest
for meaning, the essence, message, function, purpose (some terms
are at times more appropriate than others) of the work as a whole is
our ultimate ambition. We shall ask how the parts fit together, how
the parts succeed in producing the whole, and whether the whole is
supported by the parts. But at the end of the day it is the *whole*
(whether a psalm or the book of Job or the Pentateuch), *in* the
articulation of its parts, and *in* its manifold variety, that should be
the object of our quest.

This principle has been frequently neglected or positively
negated in much biblical criticism. It is still hailed as something of a
tour de force if a scholar offers an interpretation of the book of Job
that takes into account all its parts. So many chapters of the book
(the poem on wisdom, ch. 28; the Elihu speeches, chs 32—37; the
first or second divine speeches, chs 38—41; the epilogue, 42.7—17)

have been regarded by one scholar or another as secondary (i.e. not part of the original book), that the majority of interpretations of the book ignore the doubtful chapters or, indeed, interpret them in a sense at variance with the remainder of the book. The principle of the 'literary work of art', however, operates upon the fact that the book of Job, in all its 42 chapters, is what exists, and must therefore be the primary object of our interpretative scrutiny. If some parts seem hard to reconcile with other parts, we need not jump to the conclusion that the book is fundamentally at cross purposes with itself (though that is a possible conclusion, to be reached only at the end of a long and tiring road), but must seek to understand what a book so seemingly at variance with itself could possibly signify when taken as a whole.

If the thrust of the 'literary work of art' is toward 'whole' meanings rather than meanings of the parts, the dangers of the verse-by-verse interpretation, such as is followed in many commentaries and much classroom teaching, become all too clear. Unless one moves constantly between the part and the whole, the particular and the general, what appears to be a worthily thorough and detailed interpretation may in fact be a steadfast and systematic refusal to confront the primary questions of meaning.

(ii) The second emphasis of the 'literary work of art' approach, that the work should be studied primarily for what it is in itself, is common ground for a majority of critics of English literature, for example, but fairly revolutionary in biblical studies. More commonly OT scholars have insisted that an OT writing can only be interpreted in the light of history, and have gone on from there to demand the most minute historical reconstruction as a prerequisite of interpretation. Some literary critics have gone to the opposite extreme, and argued for the complete 'autonomy' of the literary work of art, i.e. that external information about the authors, their historical and social setting, their sources and the influences upon them are all irrelevant to meaning. But the more moderate statement of the American critic Cleanth Brooks would be more widely accepted, that while the interpreter needs all the help he can get from the historian, 'the poem has to be read as a poem . . . what it "says" is a question for the critic [i.e. exegete, interpreter] to answer, and . . . no amount of historical evidence as such can finally determine what the poem says'.[4]

While every scrap of external information is potentially valuable for interpretation of the OT, the surprising thing is how little is in reality significant. To understand Amos or Micah well, a paragraph or two of historical and social background probably suffices (and much more is largely guesswork); to interpret Jonah or Job it can hardly be necessary to learn about the historical origin of these books (valid though such an enquiry may be in itself), since we have no kind of certainty about such matters. To seek the 'author's intention', indeed, can lead us no deeper into the meaning of these works than to ask directly about meaning, disregarding almost entirely questions of date and authorship except on the broadest scale. The vast bulk of the data we need for interpretation is contained in the works themselves.

c. Engagement. The best interpreters of literary works are not usually those who lay claim to cool passionless detachment (which often means only the suppression of their more superficial prejudices) but those who care about the significance their interpretative work may have. Such engagement with the text does not imply any particular belief about whether the text is 'true' (whatever that may mean from time to time), but it implies concern with the question of its truth and a willingness and endeavour to reach a personal judgement. Students of Shakespeare, even at an elementary level, are called upon to discuss the character of Falstaff, the freedom or otherwise of Macbeth, the sincerity of Mark Antony, and in so doing they engage with the content of the text and with its 'truth'. And just as we may say in engaging with a fictional narrative, that it is 'true' or 'false' (or something in between), the same kind of judgements may be made of the biblical text—not indeed, with the claim of making a definitive assessment of the reality of the matter, but mainly in order to express one's own judgement of what is true or false. Genuine understanding requires evaluation; the interpreter's subjectivity is a proper element in the process of understanding, provided it does not dominate the process, and provided it allows itself to be open to correction or adjustment by the reality of the text.

The function of engagement and the process of developing understanding can be seen in any discussion of the ethics of the book of Proverbs. Suppose the question to be put is, whether the proverbs are fundamentally prudential or fundamentally religious: i.e. are the readers of the book encouraged to follow its advice because they will benefit from it, or because its advice is God's will? It is not necessary to believe in the existence of God to engage with the question; indeed it is possible that a non-believer will argue the 'religious' interpretation while a believer will argue the 'prudential' interpretation (for, from a Christian point of view the religious element in Proverbs may seem decidedly weak). Engagement means that it matters to the interpreter how the issue is resolved in that he or she has a personal stake in the issue (or some part of it). Prejudice would mean that the interpreter is concerned that the work be interpreted to suit the opinion held before interpretation began; engagement means that he or she is personally concerned with the content of the work and for that reason is concerned for its proper interpretation—at the very least, to know whether the work is a friend or a foe. Academic 'objectivity', as sometimes portrayed, would require rejection or suppression of one's legitimate interests and beliefs, and demand a concern only that the academic task be done well; engagement, which is no less steadfastly opposed to pure subjectivity and prejudice than is 'objectivity', takes seriously the human interpreter as part of the interpreting process and sets up the business of understanding as a humanizing enterprise.

B   Second-order methods

The three methods to be discussed under this heading are usually put on the same footing as those I have called 'first-order' methods. But what distinguishes the two groups is that the second-order methods principally use the biblical text for other purposes than understanding of the text. This does not mean (i) that they do not incidentally shed valuable light on the present text and so assist interpretation, or (ii) that they are not legitimate subjects of study in their own right.

a. Historical criticism.   A good deal of the OT is narrative of events; it is therefore a natural undertaking to examine how the narrated events correspond to what actually happened. Especially because much of the narrative concerns a nation and not just individuals, historians rightly regard the books of Samuel and Kings, for example, as providing the raw material for a reconstruction of Israel's history. And since the scholars best equipped to pursue such investigations are usually those who have been trained in biblical study and in OT interpretation, the impression is often given that historical study is a primary tool of OT interpretation.

Historical criticism refers to this enterprise of reconstructing the events lying behind the biblical narratives. But precisely because its focus is events and historical processes, its focus is not the biblical text and its goal cannot be the interpretation of the biblical text. Of course, everyone with an historical bent would like to know as well as possible what actually happened and would like to understand the factors behind the movements of history. But in that quest the OT becomes a source-book *for* the history; it is used as a tool, sometimes the best and sometimes only one among several, for reconstructing the past. In so far as historical criticism uses the biblical text, it is of course biblical study; but its contribution to biblical interpretation is usually indirect.

This is not to say that indirect contributions may not be very valuable. For example, every student of the OT who visits Israel and Jordan and travels through the land of the Bible finds he has acquired an almost indelible perspective from which to read the OT. The gain is not quantifiable, and one's first-hand knowledge of topography is not likely to alter any OT interpretations (though it may help to preserve one from some errors). Historical reconstruction and synthesis will have a similar type of value. No doubt the story of the conflict between twelve young warriors of David and twelve of Ishbosheth 'at the pool in Gibeon' (2 Sam. 2.12–17) is illuminated if one knows that such a pool existed, and more so if one has stood by it oneself; but the meaning of the story is hardly touched by the historical reality. Or, to take a more significant example: suppose that historical research can show, as some contemporary historians believe, that the conquest of Canaan by the Israelite tribes was really an uprising of Canaanite peasants (perhaps incited by a small band of incoming Hebrews); what difference would that make to the understanding and interpretation of the biblical narratives of the 'conquest'? In one sense, a fundamental difference, in that these narratives would be shown to be only loosely connected with historical events; in other senses, none at all, since these narratives would continue to be tales about Israel's success when obedient to God, about Israel's unity, about leadership, about conflicts within and without a group, about religious war, and so on.

So while the results of historical criticism can be fed back into biblical study and determine one dimension of the biblical texts (their relationship to what happened), they do not generally have a decisive weight in their interpretation.

b. Source criticism. This method seeks to reconstruct, not the *events* that lie behind the OT texts, but the *sources* that lie behind their contents. Such sources were both written and oral, but 'source criticism' generally refers to the reconstruction of written sources. There can be no doubt that many of the biblical texts, especially narratives and laws, were derived or adapted from previously-existing sources. Biblical writings very occasionally acknowledge their sources, as when a short poem on the 'standing still' of the sun in Joshua's time is followed by the comment, 'Is this not written in the Book of Jashar?' (Josh. 10.12–13; cf. Num. 21.14). More frequently, especially in Kings, reference is made to books where fuller detail is given (e.g. 1 Kings 11.41, 'Now the rest of the acts of Solomon ... are they not written in the book of the acts of Solomon?'); it is a fair presumption that this was the source from which the author of Kings drew his material on Solomon. In the case of the Pentateuch, though there is no specific allusion to any of its major sources, it seems necessary to suppose a complicated history of older and younger sources from which the highly variegated complex of narrative, law, and poetry was drawn.

It is sometimes supposed that the purpose of source criticism is to illuminate the final author's purpose by examining how he used his sources, what he omitted and what he retained, what he expanded or abbreviated, how he arranged the material available to him. But such studies, which we would today call redaction criticism, are rather rare compared with studies of the sources for their own sake, i.e. in order to discover what the sources *were*, and to arrange them in some sort of historical sequence. And studies of the author's use of his sources can only be effective to the extent with which we have sure knowledge of the contents of his sources. Thus within biblical studies generally the most successful application of source criticism to interpretation has been in the Synoptic Gospels—so long, that is, as it has been widely accepted that Mark was a source of Matthew and Luke. In the OT, the postulated four major sources of the Pentateuch, J E D P, are (unlike Mark) not extant, though to many scholars' satisfaction they can be reconstructed with detailed accuracy; surprisingly, however, very few scholars have used this reconstruction of the sources as a means for interpreting the text that now stands. Generally speaking, the goal of source criticism has been the sources themselves, their contents, historical settings, purposes, and interrelationships.

If we imagine the direction of source criticism changing, or of source criticism being absorbed into redaction criticism, we can conceive how source criticism could be deployed in the service of interpreting the literary works we now have. But even so, it needs to be said that many of the certainties among former generations of source critics are now increasingly called into question; and if we cannot now find agreement on the profiles of J E D and P, we are so much further from using them to interpret the Pentateuch in its final form.

Perhaps the most satisfying application of source criticism in OT studies has been in the discrimination between source material and editorial material in the Deuteronomistic History. Here it is not so much the detection of the historian's sources that is valuable for interpreting his work, but the isolation of those passages in which he is not following any source but freely composing and therefore expressing his own ideas and theological outlook.

c. Form criticism. While historical criticism attempts to reach behind the biblical text to reconstruct the history of Israel, form criticism reaches back to the oral folk literature of Israel. Its principles are these: that embedded in the written literature of a people are samples of their earlier oral literature, and that many literary forms (legends, hymns, laments, and so on) had in the oral stage a particular function in the life of the people (a life-setting; German *Sitz im Leben*). In gospel studies, form criticism sought to recover the early Christian preaching in which the narratives of Jesus' sayings and acts were recounted and took on fixed shapes. In OT studies, form criticism was fruitfully applied to the Psalms, each type of psalm (thanksgiving by an individual, hymn of praise, appeal by the community, etc.) being shown to belong to a certain type of occasion in Israelite worship. Narratives were also designated as 'aetiological saga' (a tale purporting to account for the origins of a custom or a place), 'legend' (a tale about a holy man, holy place or sacred custom that points a moral), and so on.

In that form criticism is concerned with classifying types of literature within the biblical texts (e.g. prose and poetry and their subdivisions), it performs a valuable service: by enquiring after the typical it highlights what is individual in any piece of literature, and by identifying the type or genre of the passage in question (as hymn, prophetic speech, instruction, family saga) it offers a major interpretative key to the passage. (We would be hard pressed to interpret the story in Judg. 9.8–15 about the trees' attempt to anoint a king over them until we recognized that it was a 'fable'!) But in that it 'attempts to recover the full, living history of Old Testament literature, especially to gain insight into its oral stage of development, and to place all the stages of development into their settings in the life of Israel',[5] its goal is not the interpretation of the biblical text.

It is as well to bear in mind also the provisional (not to say speculative) nature of much form criticism, as well as of much source criticism. This is no objection to the disciplines as such, but merely a reminder that in the field of the humanities knowledge does not have the precision that some scholars give the air of having achieved. In part our lack of precision is a defect due largely to the rather fragmentary nature of our subject matter; in part, however, it is a blessing, in that it gives room for individual perception, accords insight a higher value than labour, and engages the interpreter, whether novice or expert, as a person in the process of interpretation.

Throughout, this chapter has not been purely *descriptive* of the methods employed in OT studies but has attempted to be partly *prescriptive*. The arrangement of the chapter and especially the division into 'first-order' and 'second-order' methods reflects a deliberate re-evaluation of current methods on the basis of what was suggested at the outset as the primary aim of OT studies in the context of higher education: namely *understanding*. Students, beginning and more advanced, may find it of interest—if they agree with this statement of the primary aim—to consider to what extent their own courses of study appear to be directed to such an end.

NOTES

1   S. Kierkegaard, 'How to derive true benediction from beholding oneself in the mirror of the Word', in *For Self-Examination and Judge for Yourselves!*, tr. W. Lowrie (London & New York, Oxford University, 1941), p. 54.

2   F. R. Leavis, *Education and the University* (London, Chatto & Windus, 1943), p. 70.

3   W. Empson, *Seven Types of Ambiguity* (London, Chatto & Windus, 1930), pp. 286ff.

4   Cleanth Brooks, 'Literary Criticism', in *English Institute Essays* (New York, Columbia University, 1947), pp. 127–58 (p. 155).

5   G. M. Tucker, *Form Criticism and the Old Testament* (Philadelphia, Fortress, 1971), p. 9.

3

Old Testament History and the History of Israel

JOHN ROGERSON

It is well known that the Old Testament contains many books which deal with the history of the ancient Israelite people. Indeed, the Old Testament is sometimes criticized for containing so much history! Of the first sixteen books of the OT in their order in the English Bible (Genesis to Nehemiah—the order in the Hebrew Bible is different) only Leviticus, Deuteronomy and Ruth do not contribute substantially to the story of the Hebrews from the time of Abraham (*c*.1750?) to the end of the fifth century BC. In the remaining books of the OT, especially the prophetic books, there are sometimes allusions to historical events; for example, in Isaiah 7, the background is the attempt in 733 BC of the kings of Damascus and Samaria to force King Ahaz of Judah to make an alliance with them against the Assyrians.

In view of the fact that between a third and a half of the Old Testament is directly concerned with Israelite history, it is not surprising that many university and college syllabuses contain courses dealing with the historical traditions of the OT in one way or another. Such courses are valuable in providing the historical framework in terms of which the literature and theology of the OT can be studied.

These OT historical traditions are usually studied with the help of modern text-books entitled *The* or *A History of Israel*. But such textbooks are not a retelling of the biblical story in the words of modern scholars; they present the facts of OT history in a way that at some points differs radically from the biblical account. And this undoubtedly creates difficulties for many students.

Even in a comparatively conservative book such as J. Bright's *A History of Israel*,[1] the beginner will find the following deviations from what is apparently the biblical presentation: Sennacherib is said to have campaigned twice against Hezekiah, in 701 BC and in 689 BC, whereas on a straightforward reading of 2 Kings 18.13— 19.37 there was only one campaign. Bright, in fact, maintains that 2 Kings 18.13—19.37 'telescopes' *two* separate campaigns. Dealing with a later period of OT history, Bright argues that Nehemiah was active in Judah in the second part of the fifth century BC a few years earlier than Ezra, whereas the biblical view is clearly that Ezra came first (cf. Ezra 7.7 with Nehemiah 2.1).

A more radical approach can be found in M. Noth's *The History of Israel*,[2] especially in the treatment of the earliest period. Noth does not begin where the OT begins the history of the Hebrews— with Abraham (Genesis chs 1—11 deal with mankind before there were separate peoples and nations, cf. Genesis 10—11); he begins with the settlement of the Israelites in Canaan in the period after 1200 BC. He has a good reason for doing this. He is writing the history of Israel, and he believes that the name 'Israel' was first borne by a confederation of tribes in Canaan in the twelfth century BC. But Noth also believes that the basic framework of the story of the Hebrews before the settlement is unhistorical. That the patriarchs Abraham, Isaac and Jacob lived in Canaan, that their descendants went down to Egypt and that having escaped at the Exodus they wandered in the wilderness, and that they then occupied the land of Canaan—this framework he believes to be unhistorical. He does not deny that some Hebrews escaped from Egypt, or that some other Hebrews spent time in the wilderness south of Judah. But he believes that the basic framework: Patriarchs—Oppression in Egypt—Exodus—Wilderness wander-ings—Conquest, as the story of what happened to the Hebrews as a whole, is an artificial (unhistorical) framework, which crystallized in the process of the formation of the tribal confederation in Canaan.

Noth's views of the origin of the earliest traditions of the OT, those found principally in Genesis 12—50 and Exodus 1—19, and the historical reconstruction which he bases upon these traditions, are so radically at variance with what the OT recounts that this section of his *History* is likely to produce a strong reaction even from students who are in no way opposed to a carefully critical handling of the OT. They might well ask if it is really possible, on the basis of the only evidence that we have (the OT text), to reconstruct with such certainty an historical account which differs so radically from that evidence. The negative reaction of others may be based upon one or more of the following considerations.

First, we may feel that we want to stand up for the OT; not for any particular doctrinal reason, but out of loyalty to an old institution that we do not want to see mishandled. It may be that we enjoyed the stories from the OT when we were young, and that we do not want to part easily with what once provided us with enjoyment and excitement. If this is our basic reason for negative reactions to historical scholarship, then I hope to show that it is possible to accept the results of historical research, and that these results will lead us to a better appreciation of the OT stories as they stand.

Second, our objections may have moral or theological grounds. If we argue that the facts were different from what the biblical writers say (e.g. if we argue that Nehemiah came before Ezra when the OT says the opposite) are we not accusing the biblical writers of either incompetence or dishonesty, and is this not unfair since they are unable to defend themselves? The theological objections take on an even more serious tone. If the Bible is assumed to be the work of God, then it is God the author who is being charged with incompetence or dishonesty. If it is admitted that the Bible contains mistakes in its presentation of history, how can we be confident about its accuracy when it describes the works and words of God?

In my experience, many students use phrases such as 'inspired' or 'word of God' without having had the opportunity to think about their meaning. The first encounter with the historical critical method is thus as much an opportunity to begin the theological exploration of terms such as 'inspired' as it may be the occasion for a certain amount of unease. The basic issue can be put quite simply. *Either*, we define terms such as 'inspired' or 'word of God' in such a way as to claim a privileged status for the Bible so that it cannot be subjected to the kind of criticism that we would think reasonable for any other book; *or*, we allow the Bible to be studied critically and lay our view of inspiration open to what critical study may yield. The second alternative sounds very much like compromise, like chipping away at theological beliefs until nothing is left. The process can be described differently, however. We can say that by admitting the findings of critical study to the other considerations that make up our total view of inspiration, we are arriving at a truer understanding of inspiration, one purged of notions that do not rightly belong to it.

Nothing that I can write here is likely to convince those whose view of inspiration sets limits against what critical scholarship may attempt. There is, however, one point to be made. This is that there is only one place where a decision about the relation of critical scholarship to beliefs about biblical inspiration can be reached, and that is in the text of the Bible itself. So long as we do not study the text closely, we can have ding-dong battles about inspiration and biblical criticism. Discussions that take place well away from the biblical text, whether in treatises on systematic theology or in differing presentations of the history of Israel, tend only to convince the already converted. It is essential for the beginner to study a text (e.g. 1 Samuel) closely and carefully, so that he or she becomes fully aware of the genuine problems that it raises and, in the light of this study, re-examines his or her beliefs about inspiration, whatever they may be.

So far, these remarks have discussed the objection that critical scholarship is ruled out by the fact that the Bible is inspired. There remains outstanding the objection that critical scholarship in effect accuses God or the human biblical authors of inaccuracy or dishonesty. Insofar as God is brought in to the matter, it has to be asked what is implied in the claim that God is the author of the Bible. We are really back with the question of inspiration. Almost nobody today would subscribe to dictation theories of inspiration. Almost all would allow that if God inspired the biblical writers, he did not interfere with their personalities or with their distinctive gifts, but rather used these to advantage. Critical scholars who believe in inspiration would go further and say that God also allowed himself to be bound by the possibility that, as humans, the biblical writers could make mistakes; so we are back essentially to what I called the moral question, that of appearing at times to accuse the biblical writers of incompetence or of dishonesty.

In any use of the historical method today, the cross-checking of sources for our evidence is an essential part of the procedure. The fact is that memories are not always reliable. It is well known that eye-witness accounts of campaigns in the Second World War by generals who fought them are not always accurate when checked against official communiqués or telegrams or reports of the period. Further, when a modern historian pieces together a narrative on the basis of information that may have gaps, he has to make guesses. Discoveries subsequent to his work may show the guesses to have been incorrect. If to remember incorrectly is a sign of incompetence or dishonesty, then many distinguished generals have been incompetent or dishonest. If to make guesses about what happened in history, guesses which are later shown to have been incorrect, is a sign of incompetence or of dishonesty, then many historians, including historians who have tried to reconstruct the history of Israel, have been incompetent or dishonest. In fact, anyone who is engaging in the serious writing of history knows that he is taking the risk of making mistakes.

There is a further important point to make here. When a later historian corrects the work of an earlier historian, he does not necessarily show himself to be a 'better' historian. A nineteenth-century historian may have worked only from medieval manuscripts that were preserved in libraries all over Europe which he had to visit, well before the days of photocopying. A present-day historian may benefit from having a book or books in which all those manuscripts plus several that have come to light more recently are reproduced, together with commentaries and critical notes written by experts. Just because the modern historian possesses far more sources of information than did historians of one hundred years ago, it does not follow that he is 'better' than his nineteenth-century counterpart. The nineteenth-century historian may have possessed a much sounder historical judgement, and greater flair for writing historical narrative than his modern representative.

Similarly, when the modern scholar produces reconstructions of biblical history that differ from what the Bible says, he is not showing himself to be 'better' than the biblical author. The modern scholar has available so many aids that were unknown to the biblical writer. For example, the modern scholar possesses historical records of the empires of Assyria and Babylon from the ninth to the sixth centuries BC. These are centuries during which life in Israel and Judah was dominated by the expansion of these empires towards and into Syria and Palestine. It is no exaggeration to say that modern scholarship knows far more about that part of the ancient world in which the Hebrew people lived than the Hebrews could ever have known themselves. This in no way makes the modern scholar superior to the biblical writer. He is, rather, grateful for the opportunity that he has to study the OT in the light of such enlarged knowledge.

At this point, it may be worth considering what we can guess about how the biblical authors wrote their histories. We are on firmest ground for the period beginning with the reign of Solomon (*c.*970–930). After David's victory over neighbouring peoples enabled Israel to enjoy peace and security and necessitated the establishment of some sort of civil service, conditions were right for the keeping of official records. The OT mentions 'The Book of the Acts of Solomon' and the 'Chronicles of the Kings of Judah and Israel'. What these contained we do not know. It is possible that they recorded the principal events of each year of a king's reign. Other records that were probably kept dealt with the revenues of the palace and of the temple.

The Books of Kings, covering the period from the death of David (*c.*970) to the later period of Jehoiachin's imprisonment in Babylon (560 BC) are largely based upon these sources. If the 'Chronicles of the Kings of Judah and Israel' were indeed simply records of principal events for each year, then the biblical writers used their historical judgement and imagination in selecting some of these events, and in turning them into an historical narrative. It is also the case that they tried to express in their narrative their religious belief that God had been involved in the events of those years, sometimes bringing prosperity, sometimes punishing his people through misfortune.

For the period before the time of Solomon, we are much less certain about the sources used by the biblical authors. Clearly, a good deal of the material was oral tradition—stories passed from generation to generation by word of mouth. But this leaves much unexplained. Were the traditions preserved by 'guilds' of folk-singers or were they preserved by priests at local sanctuaries or by both? At what stage were they written down, and did traditions exist alongside each other in oral and written form? These are questions that cannot be answered with any certainty, although it is likely that the Exodus deliverance was first commemorated in hymns of praise to God. Whatever may have been the sources available for the period before Solomon, it is clear that the biblical writers were determined to take the story of the Hebrew people back as far as they could. In writing about a period at least several centuries before their time (I am assuming that they worked, at the earliest, in the reign of David, and probably later than that) they are likely to have made guesses and to have 'telescoped' periods.

In the treatment of the period of the Judges (1200–1020 BC), they almost certainly *expanded* the period by assuming that twelve 'judges' had operated one after the other over a period of some four hundred years. In reality, two or three of the 'judges' may have been active simultaneously in different parts of the country, while the frequent occurrence of forty years as the period for a 'judge's' rule indicates a generation—in reality more like twenty years. Although this sort of attempt to provide a basic framework for the book of Judges seems crude to the modern scholar, I do not believe that it differs in principle from the sort of guesswork that the modern historian attempts when he tries to work fragmentary evidence into a plausible historical account.

For the period after 560 BC, the biblical writers were worse off for sources than they had been for the history of the previous four hundred years. A probable reason for this is that Jerusalem was no longer an administrative capital where records were kept. Judah was part of a province governed from Samaria or Rabbat Ammon. Apart from the personal recollections of Nehemiah, who was appointed governor of Judah by Artaxerxes I in 445 BC, historical allusions to the period 519–516 BC in the prophetic books of Haggai and Zechariah 1—8, and extracts from official Persian records in the book of Ezra, there was little to go on. In describing the work of Ezra, the biblical writers may have drawn extensively upon what Nehemiah claims to have done. This would be reasonable, given the belief of the biblical writers that Ezra and Nehemiah were roughly contemporary. The authors of the Books of Chronicles wrote a history covering the period from the time of Saul (1 Chron. 10) to the return from exile (539 BC) from a priestly point of view. They used as a source the Books of Samuel and Kings, together with supplementary material whose origin is unclear and whose reliability is a matter of debate.

This brief attempt to consider what historical resources were available to the biblical writers and how they might have used them, may serve two purposes. First, it may help us to appreciate that the histories in the OT came into being in much the same way as all histories do: by the collecting of sources and the writing of historical accounts on their basis. Second, it may help to bridge the cultural gap that exists between ourselves and the OT period.

I have been insisting that although the biblical writers had far fewer resources than we enjoy, and did not have the sense of critical evaluation of evidence that we have developed comparatively recently, none the less they were not acting differently from us in principle. I propose to develop this with regard to the idea of history as explanation.

One of the tasks of the modern historian is to explain a state of affairs by giving an account of what led up to it. Why did Britain declare war on Germany in September 1939? One answer is because Germany did not reply to the British demand to cease hostilities against Poland. However, this cannot be seen in isolation from what preceded it, at least as far back as the end of the First World War. Thus a modern historian may present an account which, beginning with the 1914–18 war, explains and leads up to the German invasion of Poland, the immediate cause of the British declaration of war in 1939.

In the OT we find similar attempts to explain a situation in terms of what preceded it. Why was Jerusalem destroyed by the Babylonians in 587 BC? One answer is that Zedekiah, whom Nebuchadnezzar put on the throne when he first captured Jerusalem in 597, rebelled against his overlord. However, this is not the whole story, and it is one of the purposes of the Books of Kings to explain the fall of Jerusalem by describing what led up to the events of 587, over many centuries.

But at this point there is a most significant difference between the biblical account and what a modern historian would attempt. The biblical writer describes the events that led up to the fall of Jerusalem in 587 in order to indicate that it was the punishment of God upon his people. Some modern historians might attribute the fall of a nation to its moral laxity; none would attempt to explain it in terms of a divine purpose. It could be argued that the reason for this difference was that the biblical writer was unaware of secular forces such as economic or political pressures, and that he tended to attribute everything to God. We must notice, however, that at the time of the fall of Jerusalem there was another factor present, which the modern historian would regard as quite outside his terms of reference: a prophetic factor.

During the siege of Jerusalem, the prophet Jeremiah maintained that the city would fall, and that only surrender to the enemy would save it. God, declared Jeremiah, was on the side of the Babylonians fighting against the city that was believed by its inhabitants to enjoy God's special protection. This preaching of Jeremiah brought threats against his life, and only with difficulty did he survive to witness what he had proclaimed. Among his opponents had been other prophets who had forecast victory for Judah. The explanation of the fall of Jerusalem in the Books of Kings in terms of what led up to it is also a prophetic interpretation—an interpretation based upon the insights of a tiny group of people who stood in an intimate relationship to God which was often terrifying for themselves and embarrassing for their hearers. It would be wrong to suggest that *all* history writing in the OT is as closely bound up with prophetic witness as is the fall of Jerusalem with Jeremiah. But this particular example indicates at its sharpest the real difference between biblical history and modern history. The latter would regard interpretation of events in terms of divine intention as outside its terms of reference.

What is true of the modern historian is true also of the biblical scholar. He does not claim to have *prophetic* insight into why events took place as they did in OT times. If he is convinced that sometimes he can reconstruct the course of events with more accuracy than did the biblical writer, he knows that he can never be in a position to make judgements about the claim of the biblical writers that they could discover a divine intention in a pattern of events.

But this brings us to a very serious question which not only may worry beginners in OT studies, but which certainly divides even critical scholars. If biblical writers could have been wrong about the exact sequence of events, how can we take seriously their claim to discover a divine purpose in them? If the events did not happen, or happened differently from how the biblical writers believed, how can there have been a divine intention in them?

In trying to answer this, we must distinguish between at least two possible ways in which divine intention might be discerned in events: the direct and the indirect. A good example of the direct would be Jeremiah's involvement in the fall of Jerusalem. There was nothing built in to the complex of events that we call the fall of Jerusalem, that indicated irresistibly that it was God's will that the city should fall. Jeremiah's witness to this effect was not well received. But he was directly involved in the events, and declared with prophetic conviction what he believed to be their significance from God's point of view.

By the indirect way of discerning divine intention, I mean the possibility that someone far removed in time from the events he was considering, and entirely dependent upon oral or written traditions, could see a pattern in the events which suggested a divine intention. He might then so edit, or arrange, the materials, as to emphasize that divine intention. In so doing, he might be dependent upon information that was in part unreliable, though he could not have known that it was unreliable. He might have introduced what the modern scholar would see as distortions, although he would not have been aware that he was deliberately distorting anything. Thus, paradoxical as it might seem, it is possible to accept that compared with modern historical reconstruction, OT accounts of happenings may contain inaccuracies, but that this does not invalidate the OT claim to have discerned a divine intention in the events.

Put into other words, modern historical study of the OT is not an attack upon the integrity of the biblical writers. It does not set out from the assumption that everything in the OT is false unless it can be proved to be true. If the critical scholar comes to the conclusion that the course of events was not exactly as presented in the OT, this is only because he or she has access to materials and methods not known to the OT writers. If the beginner can come to terms with this, then he or she will have negotiated one of the most difficult stumbling blocks to serious OT study.

At the same time, the beginner must not accept uncritically everything that he or she meets in critical scholarship. Especially in reconstructions of the earliest history of the Hebrews, i.e. before the time of David, modern scholarship differs from the biblical presentation not so much because it has superior historical evidence, but because of its confidence in the form-critical and traditio-historical methods. Personally, I am sceptical about the possibility of using them as tools for reconstructing history. It might be better to say that in the case of the earliest history of the Hebrews, we simply do not know in any detail what is the relation between the biblical traditions and the events which they reflect.

To sum up this chapter: the Old Testament does not contain the history of ancient Israel. It contains historical and story-like traditions whose primary purpose is to express the faith of the authors of the OT that God had been involved in the events of the Israelite history. This material *can* be used by modern scholarship to reconstruct the history of Israel, in conjunction with texts and archaeological findings from the ancient world.

The history of Israel, as reconstructed by a modern scholar, can shed light on parts of the OT. There are historical events that are alluded to in prophetic books, but not mentioned elsewhere in the OT. For example, Isaiah 20.1–6 is probably to be connected with a revolt by Judah and other small states against Assyria in 713–711 BC; but this revolt is only known to us from sources outside the OT. Again, we know more about King Omri than the OT tells us in 1 Kings 16, since he is mentioned in several extra-biblical sources. These latter give us an idea of the immense political and economic skill of Omri, a king who took over a weak and divided country and rapidly transformed it into the most powerful small kingdom in the region. It is all the more remarkable that the biblical writer deals with him in a few verses, and comments primarily on the fact that, from the religious viewpoint, he was a very evil king.

Any scholar who writes a *History of Israel*, or who lectures on the subject, is not producing something that is intended to replace the historical traditions of the OT. He is not writing his own version of the OT. Indeed, his reconstruction will need to be corrected and improved in the light of further research. The historical traditions of the OT can never be replaced, because they are part of a witness to faith in the God of Israel, faith that arose in deeply religious circles in ancient Israel. Their primary purpose is not to provide source material for modern historians but to express faith in the God of Israel. Nothing that critical scholarship can do to the OT can call into question the fact that this faith in God existed, and was expressed in the OT historical traditions. The existence of this witness to faith is a challenge to the faith, or lack of it, of modern man. It is possible both to acknowledge that challenge, and to treat the traditions in which it is expressed, honestly and critically.

NOTES

1 J. Bright, *A History of Israel* (3rd edn London, SCM, 1981; Philadelphia, Westminster, 1981).

2 M. Noth, *The History of Israel* (2nd edn London, Black, 1972; New York, Harper, 1960).

4

The World-View of the Old Testament

JOHN ROGERSON

In the preface to this book, it was stated that the essays hoped to fulfil the same role in relation to the OT as a travel guide does when you visit a foreign country. This is especially true of the present chapter. The people of the OT used a language very different from our own. They lived in an area of different climate and terrain compared with our own. Above all, they lived a very long time ago—roughly 3,700 to 2,100 years ago. Although, thanks to modern discoveries, we know a great deal about the ancient Near or Middle East, we must avoid two extremes in considering how ancient Israelites saw and responded to the world. On the one hand, we must not exaggerate the differences between them and modern man, with the result that we create an uncrossable gulf. On the other hand, we must not imagine that the cultural differences were slight and unimportant. It is a fact that even if we have little knowledge of the cultural conditions of ancient Israel, much of the OT is still perfectly intelligible. But greater knowledge of the cultural background brings appreciation of points that would otherwise be missed.

This chapter will deal with the world of nature, magic, miracles, sacrifice and social organization. However, a word of introduction to these separate treatments is necessary.

In the chapter on the Individual and the Community, Paul Joyce warns against the making of generalizations about ancient Israelites, especially about how they thought. He rightly points to the diversity to be found in the OT. In this chapter, it will be impossible to avoid the impression that his warnings are being ignored. What this chapter attempts to describe, however, is not an entity that can be labelled 'the ancient Israelite mind'. Rather, the intention is to present something of the general framework, or shared cultural assumptions, within which the diversity of Israelite thinking took place.

The big difference between ancient Israelites and ourselves was in the way in which boundaries were drawn. For example, we make no distinctions between 'clean' and 'unclean' birds, animals and sea creatures. In the OT this is a most important distinction. Not only does it regulate what may and what may not be eaten, it regulates what may and what may not be sacrificed. But it goes further than this. It is part of a way of looking at the natural world in which this world is divided into definite spheres. In Genesis chapter 1, these spheres are identified as sky, land and sea, each with creatures appropriate to the sphere. There is some evidence that the 'unclean' creatures do not fit exactly into any sphere. For example, locusts fly but have four legs (cf. Leviticus 11.20). It is not possible to explain all the 'unclean' creatures in this way, but there can be no doubt that the distinction between 'clean' and 'unclean' creatures reflects shared Israelite assumptions about order in the world of nature, and that by observing rules about contact with 'clean' and 'unclean' creatures, Israelites were ordering their lives in conformity to a coherent set of symbols.

As will be pointed out in the section on sacrifice, the distinction between 'clean' and 'unclean' is at the heart of the way in which boundaries were established in what we would call the moral and ritual spheres. The purpose of sacrifice was to enable those boundaries to be crossed when occasion demanded, for example, when a person became a priest and thus became identified with the realm of the 'holy'; and for the boundaries to be restored when they had been violated. It is probable that ancient Israelites were much more conscious than we are about the importance of different roles in society, and that boundaries between roles were clearly marked. It is difficult to know what the coronation of a monarch signifies in modern societies where there are still monarchs (e.g. in Britain). Perhaps such ceremonies are simply opportunities to indulge in pageantry and merry-making. It is likely that in ancient Israel a coronation played a much more definite role in placing the monarch in that sphere of reality that belonged properly only to monarchs. In the sphere of the family and of social relationships, Israelites were undoubtedly much more aware than we are of the network of kinship relationships in which they were located. In a society where the enforcement of law and order was often a local matter, the responsibility of the family or of the 'tribe', it was necessary to know who were one's kin and who were one's potential enemies. It was necessary to know on whom to rely for support in the event of conflicts between larger social units. In other words, it was necessary to be aware of boundaries separating between friend and foe, and of boundaries enclosing relatives of nearer or remoter kinship. Genealogies, of which the OT seems to contain many, were important here, although it is probable that the OT in fact has only a small portion of genealogies that must have existed. Genealogies achieved at least two things. First, they helped to mark which social groups were linked politically, and which could therefore rely on each other for aid (with the implication that to mark allies is also to make it clear who are potential enemies). Second, they could establish rights of individuals or of families to residence in particular places, or of access to particular lands or wells.

Not only were the worlds of nature and social relationships clearly marked by boundaries. So was the world of time. It is no accident that Genesis 1 describes the creation of the luminaries whose function is not only to separate day from night, but to be 'for times and seasons and for days and years' (Gen. 1.14). The observance of festivals of the new moon (1 Samuel 20.5ff) and of the sabbath, not to mention the great festivals of the agricultural year, divided time clearly between the sacred and the ordinary. Indeed, the purpose of all the boundaries, wherever they were set up, was to order the whole of life in regard to the distinction between sacred and ordinary. The Israelite who had proper regard for the boundaries could be sure that his life and that of his family was ordered according to the will of God. When boundaries were transgressed, means were provided of restoring them.

The attempt has been made here to present a picture of order—albeit a very different type of order compared with what we are used to. It is necessary to make a few remarks about discussions about ancient Israelites that appear to give the opposite impression, and suggest that Israelites lived in a somewhat mystical world in which they were unable to make some of the distinctions that are fundamental to our perception of life. Paul Joyce discusses in a separate chapter the concept of 'corporate personality' according to which Israelites could not distinguish clearly between the individual and the group to which he belonged. The purpose of the sections on magic and on miracles in the present chapter is to combat the views, first, that Israelites and their neighbours were so unscientific that they thought that any thing could influence any other similar thing (e.g. if they had the colour yellow in common) and second, that being incapable of distinguishing between what we would call normal and extra-ordinary events (miracles), they could see any happening in the world of nature as a divine event, and thus had a view of nature as a 'thou' rather than as an 'it'.[1] The view of the present chapter is that Israelites were well aware of the difference between ordinary and extra-ordinary events, that nature was not capable of producing a miracle at any moment, and access to God was not the result of a mystical perception of reality, but was mediated by the boundaries that were clearly marked in the realms of nature, morality, social organization and role, and times and seasons.

A   *The world of nature*

Israelite experience of the world of nature was considerably affected by the variations in terrain and climate to be found within ancient Israel. For example, Jerusalem is on the eastern edge of a zone that stretches to the west as far as Spain, and which contains Mediterranean fauna and flora. Yet only about a mile to the east of Jerusalem there begins a treeless wilderness, which in turn becomes desert, dropping down to over 1,000 feet below sea level at the Dead Sea. The rift valley in which the Dead Sea is found shares fauna and flora with such places as the east of the Sudan. Only six miles to the east of Jerusalem, the rainfall is less than eight inches a year—insufficient for wheat to be grown. The agricultural implications of such variations will be obvious.[2] However, ancient Israelites were aware not only of agricultural implications of the very differing types of land to which they were used. In the boundaries which they drew in order to demarcate reality, they regarded the uncultivable lands with suspicion. They belonged to the sphere of the chaotic and disordered, peopled by wild animals and demons. Humans who lived there, or who were exiled there, were not members of an ordered society.

   For Jerusalem and the hill country on which it stands, rainfall was vital for the farmer. Yet it varied considerably, and there could be years of low rainfall permitting only very poor crops. When there was very high rainfall, as seems to be the case in modern Israel every twelve years or so, this could do more harm than good. Although the land promised to the ancient Israelites is described in the OT as flowing with milk and honey (Exodus 3.8), it is clear from the OT that nature was a hard taskmaster. We are told that Abram (Genesis 12) and Elimelech (Ruth 1) were forced to leave their homes because of famine. The seven fat and seven lean years in Egypt, familiar from the story of Joseph (Genesis 37,39–47) produced a famine in Canaan, with the result that Joseph's brothers were forced to travel to Egypt to buy grain. In 1 Kings 17—18 we find descriptions of the terrible effects of a drought that lasted for several years. Agriculture could also be affected by blight and mildew (Amos 4.9) or by a plague of locusts (Joel 2.1–9). When rain came after a drought, it could cause severe damage. The NT saying of Jesus about the wise and foolish builders suggests the effects of storms and floods after a period of drought, when the earth would be no more receptive than concrete to the rains.

Because imports enable us to eat almost whatever we like all the year round, quite apart from the fact that they cushion us against the effects of bad harvests, we must not forget that in ancient Israel, crops and fruits were available only in season, and then only in quantities determined by the success or otherwise of the harvest. Grain could be stored, but usually only in sufficient quantity to guarantee a supply for the year. The grain harvest was in April–May, while in September–October, there was the fruit harvest. Like their neighbours, ancient Israelites were deeply dependent upon the yearly cycle of nature. Unlike their neighbours, they celebrated the various significant points of the yearly cycle in terms of their belief and traditions about God's saving actions on their behalf, and his demands upon them as his people. Thus the fruit harvest was linked to traditions about God's provision for his people when they passed through the wilderness on their way from Egypt to the promised land (Leviticus 23.39–43). The first fruits of the harvests were offered back to God as a recognition that his was the land and that he was the provider.

It is probable that when Israelites contemplated nature, they were made aware of the sublime: of that which was so exalted or impressive as to inspire awe and wonder. When the OT talks about God in relation to nature, it often emphasizes awe-inspiring phenomena.

The voice of the LORD breaks the cedars . . .
The voice of the LORD flashes forth flames of fire.
The voice of the LORD shakes the wilderness . . .
The voice of the LORD makes the oaks to whirl, and strips the forests
  bare . . .
The LORD sits enthroned over the flood. (Psalm 29.5–10 RSV.)

When I look at thy heavens, the work of thy fingers, the moon and the
  stars which thou hast established;
What is man that thou art mindful of him, and the son of man that thou
  dost care for him? (Psalm 8.3–4 RSV.)

The failure of the rains or of the harvest, and natural disasters such
as earthquakes (Amos 1.1) or floods, were obviously a source of
great concern to the Israelites. For the OT writers, because such
failures or disasters pointed to the sublime, to that which inspired
awe and wonder, they were indications of God's judgement upon
the people (cf. Amos 4.6–13). This view was not always shared,
however, by the ordinary people. They tended to turn to the
religion of their neighbours, a religion which was closely bound up
with the yearly cycle and which sought to influence the natural
processes by magico-religious ceremonies so that agricultural
prosperity would be ensured. The result was a clash between
prophetic religion and that of the ordinary people sometimes
supported by the monarch. 1 Kings 18 provides us with an excellent
example of such a clash, in which the prophets of Baal, who had the
support of the Queen, were confronted by Elijah. At issue was both
which God was the most powerful, and which God should have the
loyalty of the people.

Some passages in the OT, for example Psalm 104, seem to suggest
that the Israelites saw God as directly involved in all the processes
of the natural world. However, it would be unwise to regard texts
such as Psalm 104 as evidence for how Israelites perceived reality.
As has been pointed out earlier, they probably saw the natural world
as divided up into distinct ordered spheres, and they approached
God in ordered ways believed to be prescribed by him. Psalm 104 is
a religious text expressing faith in God as the creator and sustainer.
It is no more a guide to general thought processes than are modern
hymns.

An important point that should be made is that it was not always easy for faith in God as creator and sustainer to be maintained in OT times. Many of the ordinary people turned to other forms of religion because it was thought that these gave a more coherent account of life. Whatever else it was, faith in God in the OT was not a conclusion drawn from an allegedly benign and orderly universe that this universe must have an originator. OT faith in God was based upon an initiative of God into the affairs of his people that required faith that God was the creator and sustainer—even if there was much that seemed to count against this faith.

B *Magic*

The type of religion to which many of the ordinary people of Israel turned, and which was condemned by the prophets, is usually described as involving magic. As stated above, it was closely associated with the yearly cycle of nature, and it was designed to achieve agricultural prosperity. It involved what is often called imitative magic—the attempt to obtain the desired results by imitating those results in advance. Thus, the limping dances performed by the prophets of Baal in their encounter with Elijah on Mt Carmel (1 Kings 18.26) may have been attempts to imitate the descent of fire. Or the sacred prostitution which was denounced by the prophets (Hosea 2.2ff) may have been an attempt to stimulate or imitate the creative processes of nature. There is even an example of an Israelite prophet using apparent imitative magic, on the occasion on which Elisha instructed King Joash to fire arrows into the ground. The king fired only three times, and the prophet was annoyed. The arrows were victories over Syria, and the three firings would mean only three victories. Had the king fired more times, he would have won sufficient victories to defeat Syria permanently (2 Kings 13).

Because of the largely negative attitude towards non-Israelite religion and its magical elements in the OT, to write a section about magic is to discuss part of the hidden agenda of the OT. Yet some explanation is called for. Magic is often thought to be an indication of a primitive and non-scientific world-view. If people think that sacred prostitution will help crops to grow, what sort of a world do they live in? It is true that magic betrays a view of the world in which scientific knowledge is much more meagre than in the modern world; but it would be wrong to suppose that because people try to obtain results by imitation, that they live in a chaotic and disordered universe where anything that has something in common with something else can affect it.[3]

Magic must be set in the context of the boundaries that this chapter has been trying to describe. It comes into its own in situations where the boundaries are breached or blurred. For example, to be involved with the death of a member of a family is to find oneself in a boundary situation, that between life and death, and magical rites are used in many 'simple' societies in such cases. Sickness is another case where the boundary between life and death may be seen to be threatened, and where magic may be used. Since the provision of a food supply is of immense importance for the wellbeing and survival of a community, magic can be used in this circumstance also.

Those who take part in magico-religious ceremonies must not be thought of as simply trying to manipulate reality in a pseudo-scientific way. The people concerned do not neglect to carry out to the full the practical skills necessary to what they are doing. The hunter does not neglect to maintain his weapons and to keep watch over his trails; the farmer does not cease to care for his soils. Without doubt, those who perform actions which imitate or symbolize what they hope to achieve believe that there is a better chance of success than if they had not performed the symbolic actions. This, in turn, may release them from anxiety, and help them to go more effectively about their business.

It cannot be stressed too strongly that in societies such as those found among Israel's neighbours, magico-religious ceremonies were essentially corporate. In a situation where the very great majority of the people were engaged in agriculture, there was a much greater awareness of the inter-relatedness between the social and the natural worlds than we can possibly appreciate, unless we were brought up in a small agricultural community. The failure of crops, or unseasonal weather, was not simply the concern of the farmer, who would complain whatever the weather was like. It was the concern of the whole community.

The magico-religious acts that were performed in connection with the cycle of the agricultural year served to bind the people together in harmony and hope in the execution of their agricultural tasks. The ceremonies expressed and reinforced shared beliefs, and helped the people to go about their work in the context of a view of life that made sense to them. When, as often, the crops failed, this must have disturbed the more thoughtful among the people at the intellectual level. But nothing short of a major upheaval would undermine the general conviction that it was necessary to go on carrying out the magico-religious ceremonies. Magic does not suggest a chaotic view of the world. On the contrary, it functions within the order provided by the many boundaries, and it can only be got rid of by the total destruction of those boundaries and the provision of alternative ones.

The opposition of the OT writers to the practices of Israel's neighbours to which the ordinary people turned was not an opposition merely to magical ceremonies as such. It was opposition to the way in which these ceremonies interpreted the boundaries of life as a whole. In the interpretation of the boundary between ruler and ruled, and between powerful and weak, the religion of Israel's neighbours knew little of the demands of the God of Israel that the strong should defend and preserve the weak. Also, aspects of the religion of Israel's neighbours, such as sacred prostitution, were repugnant to the OT writers.

The OT writers were not saying to the ordinary people: you must carry out your work of agriculture and trust in God rather than in magic. They were warning against the total commitment to an alien interpretation of life that willingness to share in magico-religious ceremonies involved. It is only when we understand the magical component of the religion of Israel's neighbours in this way that we shall appreciate the threat which it constituted to the religion of Israel, and the vehemence with which it was denounced not only by the prophets, but in the commands in the books of Deuteronomy and Joshua that the Israelites should utterly destroy their Canaanite neighbours lest they be persuaded to serve their gods.

C   *Miracles*

The view of God of the OT writers is that he is the creator and the lord of the world of nature, and that the powers of nature are his servants (Psalm 104.1–4). At decisive points in the story of Israel as the people of God, extra-ordinary events in the world of nature abound. This is particularly so at the time of the Exodus from Egypt and the wandering through the wilderness to the promised land. The Exodus is preceded by the plagues in Egypt (Exodus 7.14–12. 32), while at the heart of the Exodus deliverance is the miracle at the Red Sea (or Sea of Reeds), when the Israelites passed over the sea unscathed and their enemies were engulfed by the waters (Exodus 14). During the wilderness wanderings there are the miracles of the provision of the quails and of the manna (Exodus 16.13–21) as well as water from the rock at Massah and Meribah (Exodus 17.1–7; Numbers 20.2–13). Extra-ordinary happenings in the world of nature are to be found throughout the OT, but they are concentrated particularly in the traditions about the Exodus and the wilderness wanderings, and in the traditions about Elijah and Elisha (1 Kings 17—2 Kings 13).

It is not the intention of this section to discuss the historicity of these extra-ordinary happenings. For a treatment of the question see J. W. Rogerson, *The Supernatural in the Old Testament*.[4] Two points are considered here. The first is whether ancient Israelites were so ignorant of scientific causes that they attributed to God what we would explain in 'natural' terms. The second is whether they found it easier than ourselves to believe that extra-ordinary events happened.

It is often pointed out that there is no word in Hebrew corresponding to our 'miracle', and that the Hebrew words translated as 'sign' or 'wonder' refer to both ordinary and extra-ordinary events. It is also pointed out that the Israelites had not formulated 'laws of nature' and that therefore they had no idea of a fixed order of nature in which extra-ordinary events were exceptions. On the face of it, there is a difference here between ourselves and the ancient Israelites. For us, reality is subject to 'laws', and extra-ordinary events 'break' these laws. We are suspicious of reports about events that break 'laws of nature', and we do not find it easy to believe in extra-ordinary events as special actions of God. Ancient Israelites, on the other hand, being ignorant of the scientific causes of many things, could easily accept accounts of extra-ordinary events, and could see in them the direct activity of God.

If this contrast between ourselves and ancient Israelites is correctly described, two conclusions might be drawn. The first is that the OT reports of extra-ordinary events as special actions of God are not to be trusted, because they derive from a people whose understanding of reality was pre-scientific. The second is that the Israelites had an advantage over us (if it is an advantage) in that they could perceive God at work in events more easily than we can.

In fact, it is probably easy to exaggerate the difference between ourselves and the ancient Israelites in this matter. There is no doubt that Israelites did not know the scientific causes of events such as eclipses and rainbows, and that they would have found it easier than ourselves to see these as special actions of God. On the other hand, they knew much about the regularities of life. They observed keenly the habits of birds and animals (Jeremiah 8.7), they knew about the special properties of plants and their products. They had developed a rudimentary technology of metals, as well as agricultural skills.. They had certainly built up a stock of practical knowledge in terms of which they were aware for most of the time which happenings were normal and which were extra-ordinary.

This is clearly borne out by the requests for signs that we find in the OT. When Gideon asked (Judges 6.36–40) that the fleece left out overnight should be wet and the ground dry, and on the second occasion that the fleece should be dry and the ground wet, he, and subsequent readers and hearers of the tradition, knew perfectly well that something normally impossible was being requested. Although there is no Hebrew word for miracle, we would be well advised to accept that ancient Israelites were aware of what we call miracles. At the various crisis-points in Israel's history the OT writers relate not normal, but extra-ordinary, events, as they express their conviction that God had been acting for his people by expressing his lordship over nature.

Was it easier for ancient Israelites to 'see' God at work in the world than it is for us? The answer at one level is that in all societies, primitive, ancient or modern, there are to be found in similar proportions sceptics, those who will keep an open mind, and the gullible who long for stories or experiences of the abnormal, and who will believe almost anything. In our own society we know that there are people who are convinced that our planet is regularly visited by beings that come from other planets or from outer space. Although any generalization here is only a guess, we should reckon with the likelihood that some ancient Israelites would have found it harder to believe in miracles than some modern people, and that some ancient Israelites would have found it easier to believe in miracles than some modern people.

The OT informs us that there were those in Israel who said 'there is no God' (Psalm 14.1) while there were others who acted as though God had no interest in the affairs of the world (Psalm 73.11). There is also the fact that has been discussed earlier, that many ordinary people found other religions more helpful than that of the God of Israel. Whatever opinions we come to hold about the historicity of the miracles narrated in the OT, we should not conclude that faith in God in the OT was the product of a pre-scientific mentality that somehow made faith in God 'easy'.

D *Sacrifice*

Of all parts of the OT, those dealing with sacrifice seem to be the most foreign to us today. We have no experience of the whole business of regular killing, dissecting, blood-sprinkling, burning and disposal of the remains of animals and birds, and we find it difficult to think what it could have meant in ancient Israel. We may think that the material dealing with sacrifice is unimportant for at least two reasons. First, if we are Christians, we believe that the death of Jesus has abolished the need for a sacrificial system such as we find in the OT. Second, we may think that sacrifice does not belong to the heart of OT religion at its best.

In some of the prophetic books, it appears to be said that God does not want animal sacrifices (Isaiah 1.12–20; Jeremiah 7.21–6; Amos 5.21–4). Then there are 'spiritualization' passages, in which it appears to be said that sacrifices of praise, thanksgiving and penitence are preferable to animal sacrifices (Psalm 51.15–17; Micah 6.6–8). It may be attractive to think that the prophets and psalmists were Puritans before their time. The fact is that no reform movement from within the religion of the OT succeeded in abolishing the sacrificial system, and this for the simple reason that sacrifice was part of a much more complex system of drawing and maintaining boundaries in ancient Israel. Sacrifice cannot be extracted from the world-view of the OT without considerable damage to the whole fabric; and the sacrificial system was brought to an end only by major upheavals from outside. The first, when the temple was destroyed by the Babylonians in 587 BC, ended sacrifices temporarily (although some scholars maintain that some sort of system continued until the rebuilding of the temple and the full restoration of sacrifice in 516 BC). The second upheaval, when the Romans destroyed the temple in AD 70, brought sacrifice permanently to an end. Sacrifice, then, was part of a system of behaviour that had such deep social roots that although it may have been subjected to violent criticism, only a major upheaval brought it to an end.

Sacrifice in the OT was a form of symbolic behaviour which enabled boundaries to be crossed, and which enabled boundaries to be restored when they had been violated. As stated earlier, the most fundamental boundary, so far as sacrifice was concerned, was that between clean and unclean. This cut right across the distinction that we make today between moral offences (the breaking of rules governing behaviour towards other human beings) and ritual offences (the breaking of rules about religious ceremonies, or about unclean objects). A person could become unclean, and thus violate the boundary between clean and unclean in many ways: by contact with a dead body (Leviticus 22.4), or with an unclean animal (Lev. 11.24–7); by contracting 'leprosy' (Lev. 13—14), by menstruating or giving birth (Lev. 12.1–8; 15.19ff), by damaging the property of another person (Lev. 6.1–7) or by breaking a divine commandment unintentionally (Lev. 5.14–19).

How sacrifice enabled boundaries to be crossed and restored is best illustrated by the ritual for rehabilitating the 'leper' in Lev. 14. On being declared a leper, a person was excluded from society. This was no doubt sound from the public health point of view. But at a deeper level, the exclusion came about because the leper had contracted a permanent form of uncleanness, and as such, could not remain inside the boundaries that divided ordered social relationships from the disordered sphere beyond. The fact that the leper had to live outside the town or village indicates the way in which the land was also thought to be ordered into spheres reflecting order and chaos.

The ritual began with the priest meeting the leper 'outside the camp' (Lev. 14.3), that is, outside the sphere of ordered relationships. An elaborate ritual, including the release of a bird which probably symbolized the removal of uncleanness, brought the leper into an intermediate state between society and outside of it. For seven days the leper lived inside the camp but outside his tent (Lev. 14.8). On the eighth day, a final elaborate ritual completed the passage back to full membership of society.

This ritual can be usefully compared with two other ceremonies. The first was that for consecrating priests in Lev. 8—9. What is common between the rituals is the seven days spent in an intermediate position. In the case of the priests, they are crossing the boundary between the ordinary and the sacred, and they spend seven days at the door of the tent of meeting, forbidden to enter the tent. They are thus part-way on their passage from the ordinary to the sacred, and they only finally enter the tent of meeting after the completion of their transition on the eighth day. The other ritual that can be compared is that for the Day of Atonement in Lev. 16. What is noteworthy here is the use of sacred space. The goat that is to bear the sins of the community is led through the camp, and out into the wilderness. Thus is symbolized the removal of uncleanness from the ordered to the chaotic, as meant by the wilderness.

This account of sacrifice, as well as concentrating upon ceremonies concerned with the removal of uncleanness and of crossing boundaries at the expense of many offerings that were designed simply to express thanks and gratitude to God, has described a view of reality that was not unique to the ancient Israelites. This view is to some extent common to all peoples who practise sacrifice. What was distinctive about OT sacrifice was the story in the context of which it was set. The whole system is presented in the OT as having been instituted by God on Mt Sinai after the Exodus. The fact that modern scholarship has shown that many elements of sacrifice were probably taken over from Israel's neighbours is not relevant here. As part of a coherent set of symbols, whatever the origin of some of those symbols, the sacrifices are given coherence and meaning by the Sinai story. The law-giving is presented in the OT as God's gift to his people after he had delivered them from slavery in Egypt. Sacrifices are thus part of the way in which Israel must respond in gratitude to God for his gracious redemption and his continuing care for the people. The sacrificial system enabled the Israelites to order their lives in loyalty to the God who had revealed himself at the Exodus. If and when they broke his laws, the sacrifices enabled relationships to be restored.

No mention has been made so far of serious offences such as murder, adultery and blasphemy, and of the sacrifices to be brought in these cases. In fact, no sacrifices were prescribed for these and similar offences because the death penalty was prescribed instead (e.g. Exodus 21.12–17). We do not know to what extent the death penalty was carried out in such cases. In the case of the family of David, David's adultery with Bathsheba was punished only indirectly (the child conceived by Bathsheba died) although he was strongly condemned, and then forgiven in the name of God by the prophet Nathan. Absalom's murder of his brother seems to have gone unpunished, apart from banishment (cf. 2 Sam. 11—13 for all these events). If execution for serious offences was carried out regularly in ancient Israel, it is likely that as in other societies, such executions involved rituals designed to indicate that when society takes the life of an individual, this is no light matter. There is a sense in which such an execution is a sacrifice in which no animal can substitute for the criminal.[5]

It is clear from the OT that sacrifices were abused; that people thought that mere observance of ritual would bring prosperity (cf. Amos 4.4–5). Perhaps a reason for this was that addiction to rival forms of religion, which did not set their rituals in the context of the story of the Exodus salvation, dulled the willingness of the people to observe the moral requirements of the God of the Exodus. Perhaps people who abused sacrifices had no feeling for sacrifice as a form of symbolic behaviour preserving boundaries and pointing to God. However, we shall understand the sacrificial aspects of Israelite life only if we concentrate not on the abuses, but upon the interrelationship that obtained in ancient Israel between sacrifice and the social and moral order.

E   *Social organization*

In spite of the fact that the OT appears to contain much information about social organization, we probably know much less about this than we might expect. The reason is that social organization was much more subject to political changes than other ways in which boundaries were drawn in ancient Israel. In this section, no more can be attempted than to describe the principal periods into which we must divide ancient Israel's history so far as it affects social organization, with indications of what we can guess about social organization in these periods. The four periods are: the period of the Patriarchs (Abraham, Isaac and Jacob), the period of the Judges, the period of the monarchy and the period of the post-exilic community.

It is widely held that Genesis 12—50 (our principal evidence for the patriarchal period) and Joshua–Judges (our principal evidence for the period of the Judges) reached their present form long after the periods to which they refer, and that they cannot be expected to supply evidence for very much about these early periods. This is only one of the problems involved in trying to write about social organization in ancient Israel. This section is not written in ignorance of the critical problems; it will try to draw out what is presented in the OT about the patriarchal period and the period of the Judges without prejudice to the historicity of the presentations.

The Patriarchs are portrayed as extended families, breeding sheep, goats and possibly camels,[6] and moving from place to place. It is common to call them semi-nomads. There is, perhaps, no harm in this, provided that it is appreciated that social and cultural anthropologists do not find the term useful.[7] We must also be on our guard against supposing that if the Patriarchs were semi-nomads, their semi-nomadism represented a point on a scale of cultural evolution according to which peoples pass through semi-nomadism from pure nomadism on their way to settled life. In fact, settled peoples can become transhumant (to use the technical term) for various reasons. They may be forced out of their settled existence by tiny alterations in climate or ecological balance that make full dependence upon agriculture impossible. They may be forced out of their settled homes by invaders (the twentieth century has many examples of this). The biblical record seems to affirm that Abraham's family had been city-dwellers (Genesis 11.31), and if this is correct, the transhumance of the Patriarchs was not simply part of natural cultural evolution.

It is difficult to know how large the patriarchal families were. On the face of it they were quite small. According to Genesis 46.27, Jacob's family numbered seventy when he went to live in Egypt. These small numbers are supported by other features of Genesis 12—50. For example, Abraham is most concerned that he should have an heir, and tries adoption (if that is the meaning of Gen. 15.2), and having a son by his wife's woman servant (Genesis 16). Had the patriarchal families been large, presumably there would have been women available who were sufficiently distant from the kinship point of view to have served as wives for Abraham. In the case of Isaac, a wife is sought from Abraham's kin who were still far away to the north east (Genesis 24), and it is from the same source that Jacob obtains his two wives (Genesis 29). On the face of it, we have small families, determined to maintain the boundaries between themselves and the local population, and consequently faced with the problem of how to obtain suitable wives. Against this picture, the enigmatic Genesis 14 tells us that Abraham put three hundred and eighteen armed servants into the field in a battle against the kings of the plain.

During the period of the Judges, ancient Israel is presented as a confederation of tribes. The familiarity of the word 'tribe' should not blind us to the fact that for social and cultural anthropologists the word tribe is problematical.[8] It has been used to describe so many different types of social organization that it has become at best meaningless, and at worst, misleading. It is often supposed that Joshua 7.14 gives us a picture of how tribes were constituted: that they were made up, in descending order of size, of families (or 'clans'), extended households, and individual male heads of what we today call nuclear families. Unfortunately, many exceptions to this neat scheme of things can be found.

We must content ourselves by saying that tribes were clearly-marked, self-contained social groups, which regulated the lives of their members according to custom and law. They were marked off from each other either by kinship or geographical location or both. They commanded the loyalty in war of all fighting males. At this period in Israel's history, a man and his family looked to the tribe to protect him from enemies outside and inside the tribe, in return for which he accepted the law and discipline of the tribe and its right to call him to battle. Individual tribes, through their elders, entered into larger tribal alliances as occasion demanded, e.g. war, or to punish a tribe that had offended grossly against another tribe (Judges 19—21).

With the establishment of the monarchy and the subsequent centralization of administration there must have been a considerable modification of the tribal organization. Conscription for military and other national service, the specialization of trades and the growth of the importance of cities must have had their effect. It is also clear that changing economic conditions made it possible for class divisions to emerge in which landowners and moneylenders could oppress the poor, seize their lands and sell them into slavery. The OT stresses the duties of closely related members of families to support each other in such times of crisis; and the need to protect the rights of widows, orphans, and aliens is also stressed. Prophetic preaching was directed particularly against the exploitation of the weak who had no family group to defend them.

The exile, in which the wealthy and powerful classes were removed to Babylon, must have had a profound effect upon ancient Israel's social organization. From the information in the books of Ezra and Nehemiah, members of the post-exilic community identified themselves as members of either families or particular villages. Various officials were in charge of districts of Jerusalem and Judah (Nehemiah 3.14ff). In some cases, there were residents who could not prove by genealogies that they were Israelites (Ezra 2.59ff).

This brief sketch will have served as an indication that the social organization of Israel underwent many modifications in the course of Israel's history. How far writings referring to earlier periods which reached their final form in times when the social organization of the earlier periods had been substantially modified, could accurately reflect the organization of the earlier periods, is a matter of debate. Readers of the OT will be well advised to bear in mind the complexity of the problems involved as they read the OT. They may also be helped by having read a simple introduction to social organization.

NOTES

1 The sort of view that I have in mind is presented in the essay 'Myth and Reality', in H. Frankfort and others, *Before Philosophy* (Harmondsworth, Penguin, 1949); complete edn, *The Intellectual Adventure of Ancient Man* (Chicago, University of Chicago, 1946).

2 An excellent discussion of the geographical significance of Galilee and Jerusalem can be found in J. Wilkinson, *Jerusalem as Jesus Knew It* (London, Thames & Hudson, 1978), pp. 17–23, 30–43.

3 For a much fuller discussion see J. W. Rogerson, *Anthropology and the Old Testament* (Oxford, Blackwell, 1978; Atlanta, John Knox, 1979), pp. 47–51.

4 J. W. Rogerson, *The Supernatural in the Old Testament* (Guildford, Lutterworth, 1976); B. Kaye and J. W. Rogerson, *Miracles and Mysteries in the Bible* (Philadelphia, Westminster, 1978).

5 See M. F. C. Bourdillon in M. Fortes and M. F. C. Bourdillon, ed., *Sacrifice* (London, Academic, 1980), p. 13. In the same volume see also the article by J. W. Rogerson, 'Sacrifice in the Old Testament: Problems of Method and Approach', pp. 45–59.

6   Camels are mentioned frequently in the patriarchal narratives (e.g. Genesis 12.16), but scholars are by no means agreed whether these references accurately reflect the state of affairs at the time of the Patriarchs.

7   On semi-nomads see J. W. Rogerson, *Anthropology and the Old Testament*, pp. 41–3.

8   On 'tribes' see *Anthropology and the Old Testament*, pp. 86ff.

FOR FURTHER READING

On genealogies: R. R. Wilson, *Genealogy and History in the Biblical World* (New Haven, Yale University, 1977).

On the world of nature and its division into spheres: Mary Douglas, *Purity and Danger* (London, Routledge, 1966); *Implicit Meanings. Essays in Anthropology* (London, Routledge, 1975), pp. 303–5. Also J. W. Rogerson, 'The Old Testament View of Nature: Some Preliminary Questions', in *Oudtestamentische Studiën*, XX (1977), pp. 67–84.

On sacrifice: the volume edited by Fortes and Bourdillon (note 5 above). On magic: Rogerson, *Anthropology* (see note 3 above).

On social structure: Rogerson, *Anthropology* (see note 7 above).

Also, C. S. Rodd, 'The Family in the Old Testament', *The Bible Translator*, vol. 18 (1967), pp. 19–26. A good general introduction to social structure is R. Fox, *Kinship and Marriage* (Harmondsworth, Penguin, 1967).

5

The Individual and the Community

PAUL JOYCE

The reader of the Old Testament cannot help being struck by the importance attached in ancient Israel to the social group or community. The important unit when dealing with morality, law and religion in the Old Testament often seems to be not so much the individual as the group to which he belongs. The Israelite looks to his family for aid and protection, particularly when his property or the continuation of his name are threatened. For example, when a man died and left a childless widow, the man's brother was expected to marry her, and the first son of this union was to succeed to the name of the dead brother, 'that his name may not be blotted out of Israel' (Deut. 25.6). Or again, if a poor man was forced to sell his property or even sell himself into slavery, a close relative was expected to act as *Goel* or Redeemer, and bail out the poor relative, so as to keep the property—or the man—in the family (Lev. 25.25, cf. vv. 39–43).

There could also be a negative side to this strong sense of community. In the case of a sin or a crime, the whole family of the man who actually committed the act could be punished, even though they had nothing to do with the offence. For example, in 2 Sam. 21, seven descendants of Saul are executed so as to remove the guilt incurred by their ancestor Saul when he put to death some Gibeonites. Or again, in Joshua 7, when Achan is executed for stealing some valuables which had been seized in battle but which had been dedicated to God, his entire family is executed with him.

In addition to his immediate family or household, the ancient Israelite usually regarded himself as belonging to an extended family. And then, more widely still, he regarded himself as belonging to one of the tribes of Israel. Finally and most importantly, the Israelite was strongly aware of being one of the

74

'Sons of Israel', the people of Yahweh, and it was above all from this sense of being part of a nation that the ancient Israelite seems to have derived his personal sense of identity.

Yahweh was first and foremost the God of the people of Israel; one might say that he was only the God of the individual Israelite in so far as the individual participated in the nation of Israel, which regarded itself as chosen for a special relationship with Yahweh. Religious experience seems normally to be viewed in the Old Testament in the broad setting of the community. It is not surprising, then, that this community of Israel seems to have relied above all on the worship of the one God, Yahweh, as the great uniting principle of its life. As Israel began to become more conscious of its unity as a nation, during the period from about 1200 to 1000 BC, it seems to have been common allegiance to one God, rather than any highly organized political organization, which gave this mixed group of people a growing sense of shared identity. And later, in the period after the Exile of Judah in Babylonia in the sixth century BC, it seems to have been worship which was the essential bond which united the people of Israel. (It is significant that the name Israel is still used in this later period to describe the worshipping people of Yahweh, even though the political entity known as Israel, the northern sister kingdom of southern Judah, had long since ceased to exist.) Israel after the Exile typically viewed itself as the holy people of Yahweh gathered around his sanctuary in Jerusalem. The boundaries of this community were made all the clearer by the emphasis placed on specifically Jewish practices such as circumcision and Sabbath observance. Those who in serious respects broke the sacred law of Moses, increasingly the focus of religious life, could be excommunicated, or expelled from the community, so as to preserve the purity of Israel as the holy people of Yahweh. Moreover, within this community of the people of Yahweh, we find worship as an essential uniting factor also for smaller groups in society. For example, the Passover was very much a family festival celebrated at home, and as such was one of the essential bonds of Israelite family life.

It may be said, then, that in ancient Israel, the community, whether the immediate family, the extended family, the tribe, or the nation itself, was of enormous importance and that there was a close link between the worshipping life of Israel and this strong sense of community. It is true to say that many aspects of this strong sense of community, particularly those relating to the punishment of sin or crime noted earlier, strike the modern reader as somewhat strange, even at times immoral. However, it should not be thought that the tendency to think in terms of a community or a corporate group is entirely alien to our experience. For example, when speaking of a committee or a football team we often tend to imply that the group involved has a kind of personality of its own. We are aware of a tension in our thinking between the corporate group and the individuals of whom it is made up; and this tension is often reflected in the inconsistency of our language, referring to the committee, for example, at one moment as 'they' and, at the next, as 'it'. Or again, in contemporary worship, it is not unknown for the prayers of the congregation to be summed up in a prayer which uses the word 'I' in a sense which is meant to represent all those present.

Despite such modern parallels to much of what we find in the Old Testament, some scholars have felt that the strong emphasis on the community in ancient Israel calls for further explanation. Some have even argued that it is to be seen as the result of a different psychology, an altogether different way of viewing the world. The best known advocate of such a theory was H. Wheeler Robinson,[1] who argued that in ancient Israel, the limits of an individual's personality were not clearly defined and that much of the Old Testament is to be understood in the light of the alleged fact that the individual was not even distinguished from the group to which he belonged. The group, said Robinson, could be thought of as having a 'Corporate Personality'. Thus, in the case of the story of Achan in Joshua 7, the guilt of the one man, Achan, extended to the group to which he belonged. At first, the whole people of Israel are defeated in battle, but later, when Achan is isolated as the culprit, his whole family is executed with him. This is appropriate, argued Robinson, because Achan's personality is thought of as extending into the group. In speaking of 'Corporate Personality' in this way, Robinson was attempting to give a rather bold psychological explanation for cases such as that of Achan. He was arguing, in large part on the basis of some of the books on anthropology which appeared in the early part of this century, that ancient Israel's thinking in this area was really that of a primitive or pre-logical people, and that only when this was recognized could the Old Testament be understood correctly. Robinson, and a number of scholars who were influenced by him, used this theory to try to explain a variety of puzzling features in the Old Testament. For example, in the central section of the book of Isaiah, we find the figure of the Suffering Servant of Yahweh. Scholars have long discussed the meaning and significance of the passages which refer to the Servant. One problem is that sometimes the Servant is spoken of as Israel (e.g. Isa. 49.3) and at other times he sounds much more like an individual (especially in chapter 53). Robinson argued that the Servant was indeed sometimes viewed as a corporate group and at other times as an individual, but he went on to give an explanation of this based on his theory of 'Corporate Personality', claiming that the ancient Israelite mind was capable of a swift transition from the one to the many, and vice versa, an ability quite unparalleled in our modern way of thinking.[2] Another feature of the Old Testament which has long puzzled scholars is the way that in many of the Psalms there is an inconsistency in the use of the singular and the plural. For example, in Psalm 44, we read in verse 4:

Thou art my King

and similarly in verse 6,

For not in my bow do I trust,

and yet in verse 5 we read,

Through thee we push down our foes

and again in verse 7,

Thou hast saved us from our foes.

Robinson felt that such inconsistency between 'I' and 'we' demanded some psychological explanation such as his theory of 'Corporate Personality'. The Psalmist, he felt, really did not distinguish the individual from the group and so slid easily from one to the other.

We must ask ourselves, however, whether the evidence of the Old Testament does indeed demand such an explanation. Scholars have suggested plausible alternative explanations for particular cases. For example, it has been suggested that the reason Achan's family is executed with him is not that his personality is thought of as extending into them in some way; rather that Achan's family are regarded as his property. Their destruction is part of Achan's punishment. Moreover, it has been persuasively argued that the anthropological studies upon which Robinson based his notion of 'Corporate Personality' are now outdated and discredited.[3] There is, however, a still more basic criticism which can be made of his theory, namely that it seems to deny to the ancient Israelite the awareness of being an individual which modern man obviously has. Robinson does in fact speak of the Old Testament as being produced 'prior to the development of the modern sense of personality', but it is by no means clear that it is appropriate or necessary to speak of ancient Israel as a 'primitive' people or of its thinking as 'pre-logical'. At no point does the emphasis on the community in the Old Testament demand that the ancient Israelites should have had a psychology essentially different from our own. We have already suggested a number of modern examples (the committee or the football team) where we tend to attribute a kind of personality to a corporate group; but no one would suggest for a moment that this is because we are unable to distinguish between groups and individuals. Why, then, should we suppose that the ancient Israelites were unable to make such distinctions? We are quite familiar with the personification of nations. For example the figure of Britannia, or of other groups, as in the case of memorials to the Unknown Soldier. When discussing history, politics or sociology, we inevitably become aware of the tension between speaking of corporate groups and social forces on the one hand and real individual human beings on the other. The complexities and tensions of the relationship between groups and the individuals of whom they are made up are an inescapable fact of human life in all ages. These are things which we share in common with the ancient Israelites rather than things which set them apart from us. Certainly, cultures differ enormously one from another (this is one of the primary lessons of all historical study) and we do feel a sense of injustice at the fate of Achan's family, wishing to regard them as innocent individuals. But the differences are not to be exaggerated; the differences between cultures are rarely absolute; they are almost always differences of degree. It is fair to say that for the most part the Old Testament does convey a stronger sense of the importance of the community and of corporate groups than we are used to, and this does give rise to what seem to us to be injustices and anomalies. But this does not mean that we should regard the Old Testament as the literature of a primitive people, totally alien to modern western thinking.

We have dwelt on H. Wheeler Robinson's theory of 'Corporate Personality' not only because of its direct importance for the question of the individual and the community in Israel, but also because it provides a salutary warning of the tendency of such scholarly notions to become taken for granted and employed somewhat indiscriminately in biblical studies. To begin with, the theory was advanced as a psychological explanation of certain perplexing passages such as that relating to Achan. Then, it came to be regarded by Robinson as an essential feature of 'Israelite Thought' as such, and soon it came to be applied by Robinson and many others to a host of passages and issues in the Old Testament, and also the New Testament. The notion of 'Corporate Personality' is occasionally vague and confusing even in Robinson's own writings,[4] but in the hands of others it was often used even more loosely. We shall see later that it is in any case always risky to speak about typical 'Israelite Thought' as something which may be precisely described (largely because Israel and its literature contain such an enormous variety of ways of thinking), but such language is even more suspect when it involves a notion as ill-founded as Robinson's 'Corporate Personality'. The new student of biblical studies would do well to be aware that fashions are as common in scholarship as in any other area of life. A notion such as 'Corporate Personality' can be like a band-wagon onto which numerous scholars jump, often ill-advisedly; and such ideas can equally quickly fall out of fashion. The student should learn to read the works of biblical scholars with a critical eye; he or she will often find different opinions being expressed and should soon acquire the ability to spot the particular axe an author has to grind. This should not be a cause of anxiety; it is part of what makes biblical studies such a rich and exciting field. Above all, students should have the courage to make up their own minds, and that is best done by balancing the reading of books about the Bible by careful reading of the biblical text itself.

Another very widely-held notion about the Old Testament, perhaps even more influential than Robinson's theory of 'Corporate Personality', is that which suggests that there was a steady, and traceable, development in Israel's thinking away from a strong emphasis on the community (such as we have considered) towards an ever-increasing emphasis on the individual. This has long been, and remains, an extremely prevalent view both in scholarly works on the Old Testament and in more popular presentations.[5] However, the basis of this notion is by no means as sound as is commonly assumed. It will be useful for us to look at this question now, not only because this should shed further light on our topic of the individual and the community in Israel, but also because such an enquiry should again highlight various more general features of Old Testament study.

The developmentalist view which we are considering envisages a shift away from the strong emphasis on the community and corporate responsibility, of which the Achan case is often cited as an example, to a situation in which each individual Israelite is held responsible for his own deeds. It is usually suggested that the crucial stage in this development was the period of Judah's Exile in Babylonia in the sixth century BC, with the words of the prophet Ezekiel usually being regarded as an especially important step in the development of individualism in Israelite thought. This long development is often seen as playing an important part in preparing the ground for the Christian revelation. However, in attempting to create a neat system, this simple theory in fact misrepresents a much more complicated set of facts. To begin with, an important distinction needs to be made between, on the one hand, language about criminal law on the human level and, on the other hand, language about God's punishment of human sin. In criminal law, a crime is committed and eventually, when the culprit has been detained and found guilty, the appropriate punishment is imposed. In Deuteronomy 24.16, in a legal passage, we read, 'The fathers shall not be put to death for the children, nor shall the children be put to death for the fathers; every man shall be put to death for his own sin'. In its present form, this verse probably comes from the seventh century BC, but most scholars concede that, in the area of Israel's criminal law, the general principle from the earliest times seems to have been that justice demanded that the individual responsible for a crime should be isolated and punished. The situation is rather different, however, when we turn to consider language about God's punishment of human sin. It is here that we find the strongest tendency to think in terms of whole groups of people being responsible and being punished; and the reason is not difficult to see. Ideas about God punishing human sin tend to start from the experience of hardship or suffering which call for explanation. A common explanation for hardship in ancient Israel, as in many other cultures, was that God must be angry and must be punishing wrongdoing. However, in these circumstances it was often difficult to identify the particular wrong in question, and so the tendency was to think in general terms of the group or of all Israel as a people having displeased God. Moreover, where even this did not seem to offer a satisfactory explanation for the hardships being suffered, a longer-term view could be taken. One could explain present suffering which was apparently undeserved by looking back in history to some notorious sin which could be seen as the cause of God's wrath. Thus, for example, when the authors of the Books of Kings (see 2 Kings 23.26–7) attempted to account for the great disaster of 587 BC, when Babylonia destroyed the Jerusalem temple and exiled many Judeans, they looked back to the notorious sins of Manasseh, who had been King of Judah in the seventh century BC. And so it is that we find the idea of inherited guilt; Israel is thought of as a community extending through history, and the generation alive in 587 BC can be thought of as being punished for sins which, strictly speaking, they did not commit. We must remember, then, that when we ask questions about how responsibility was understood in Israel, the situation is likely to vary according to the area of responsibility being discussed, and that the stronger emphasis on group responsibility is likely to be found mainly in the area of language about God's punishment of sin.

However, the even more basic point to grasp is that it seems that throughout Israel's history and literature, we find a combination of both communal and more individualistic elements in language about responsibility. Even in the area of language about God's punishment of sin we find at an early date some feeling that it was somehow unsatisfactory to envisage Yahweh acting in history in a way which was less fair than the normal practice of Israel's criminal law, where the general principle at least was that the guilty man should be the one to be punished. So, for example, in Genesis 18, possibly written as early as the tenth century BC, Abraham pleads with Yahweh not to punish the righteous people of Sodom along with the wicked. In verse 25, we read:

> Far be it from thee . . . to slay the righteous with the wicked . . . Shall not the judge of all the earth do right?

Moreover, just as here we find, early in Israel's history, a concern for the fair treatment of the righteous individual, we also find in the very late period of Old Testament times a certain amount of language which envisages those who, strictly speaking, are innocent being included in the punishment of the guilty. For example, in Daniel 6.24, when Daniel's wicked accusers are cast into the den of lions, the same fate befalls their children and their wives. Even in the New Testament we find some examples of the notion of inherited guilt mentioned earlier. In Matthew 23.35, Jesus is portrayed as foretelling that upon the scribes and Pharisees of his own day will come

all the righteous blood shed on earth, from the blood of innocent Abel to the blood of Zechariah the son of Barachiah.

The simple developmental theory which pictures a steady growth in Israelite thought from communal responsibility to individual responsibility does not do justice to such evidence.

Even within a single passage in the Old Testament we often find a complex combination of communal and individualistic elements. For example, in the story of Achan in Joshua 7, at first all Israel suffers defeat in battle because of Achan's sin, which suggests a strong emphasis on Israel as a group. Joshua then sets about discovering the guilty person, clearly a much more individualistic concern; and yet when Achan is isolated and punished, all his family are executed along with him. Genesis 18 provides another example of such complexity. We have seen that Abraham pleads with Yahweh not to include righteous individuals in the general destruction of Sodom; and yet the solution which is proposed is that if ten righteous be found, the whole city should be spared, an idea which seems to reflect a tendency to think in terms of the community as the really important unit. These two passages, then, each seem to combine a variety of ways of viewing responsibility. They also illustrate another important point. So much of the evidence with which we have to deal in the Old Testament is in story form. Such stories were not intended to present a systematic theology, and though they are of help to us in our study of ideas and beliefs held in Israel, we would be very foolish to try to extract from such materials an Israelite theology of responsibility.

As was mentioned earlier, the work of the prophet Ezekiel has often been taken to represent a particularly important stage in the alleged steady development from a communal to an individualistic emphasis in Israel's thinking about responsibility. Ezekiel has been regarded as the great prophet of individualism, his teaching in the first half of the sixth century marking the crucial turning point away from the old ideas of corporate responsibility and towards the supposedly new truth of individual responsibility. However, this is a misrepresentation. As we have seen, there were important elements of individualism in thought about responsibility in Israel from an early date, certainly earlier than Ezekiel's work in the sixth century BC. It is, moreover, in any case by no means clear that Ezekiel was concerned to stress individual responsibility. Chapter 18 of the book of Ezekiel is the chapter most often cited by those who would claim that individualism is a prominent feature of Ezekiel's teaching. An examination, albeit brief, of that chapter will provide an illustration of the necessity, when considering issues like this, to ask especially carefully what a particular chapter is saying.

A careful reading of chapter 18 of Ezekiel reveals that Ezekiel's purpose is not to argue that particular individuals will be judged in isolation from their contemporaries. His concern is not with individuals at all. Rather, he addresses the house of Israel in a national crisis, the subjugation of Judah by Babylonia and the exile of many of her people. This catastrophe inevitably affected the whole nation, and so it is the house of Israel as a community which Ezekiel exhorts to make the appropriate response. He says they are no longer to blame the sins of their ancestors for the present situation. They are not to use the proverb, 'The fathers have eaten sour grapes and the children's teeth are set on edge' (vv. 2–3). Here Ezekiel criticizes the idea of inherited guilt which we mentioned earlier; the present generation must, he says, recognize its own responsibility and repent. It is very important to note (the point is often missed) that in rejecting the idea of inherited guilt, Ezekiel does not attempt to put in its place a theory of individual responsibility. Rather, he calls on the present generation to stop blaming past generations and, as the community of the house of Israel alive today, to turn to Yahweh in repentance.

To illustrate his point, Ezekiel pictures three men: a righteous man, his wicked son and his righteous grandson (Ezekiel 18.5–18). Ezekiel appeals (in v. 20) to the general principle, which, as we have said, seems to have been the working basis of Israel's criminal law from early times, namely that it is the guilty man who should be punished. Accordingly, it is said that the righteous man shall live and that the wicked son shall die, despite his father's righteousness. Then we come to the really crucial case. Ezekiel says that the righteous grandson shall live; he shall not die for his father's sins. It is vital to note that Ezekiel is here giving an illustration of the situation of the nation Israel in its present crisis in history. His point is that the present generation which is suffering conquest and exile must be suffering for their own sins; if they were righteous they would not be suffering. It is easy enough to see how this section of chapter 18, picturing the three men, could be misread as an argument for individual responsibility. Certainly, it takes for granted and appeals to the general principle of individual responsibility as normally applied in criminal law (i.e. it is the guilty man who should be punished), but when we read this section of the chapter in the context of the chapter as a whole it becomes clear that Ezekiel is addressing a given historical situation and answering the question why the nation is suffering as it is.

Ezekiel's purpose in all this is very positive: he wishes to persuade his audience of their responsibility so that he can challenge them to repent. In the section beginning at verse 21, he stresses that if a wicked man repents, his past will be forgotten, and that if a righteous man falls into sin, he will not be spared punishment on account of his previous righteousness. Again all this relates to the situation of the nation Israel, Ezekiel's point being that if the community, acknowledging its responsibility and its sin, repents, it will not be punished for its previous sins. The present generation of Israel is not only free of the punitive effects of the sins of past generations; but more, the community may even become free of the punitive effects of its own past sins. The whole argument of chapter 18 is presented very subtly by Ezekiel to lead his audience into a position where they may respond to his very positive challenge to 'turn and live'. We know from chapter 9 that Ezekiel was not altogether unconcerned about the fact that some innocent people might suffer in the present crisis, but for the most part he really does not concern himself with this problem, because his primary task is to address and explain a given disaster affecting the nation as a whole, a disaster which he can even describe, in a rhetorical phrase, as cutting off 'both righteous and wicked' (Ezekiel 21.3). This is a strange phrase indeed to find in a book so often seen as representing the crucial stage in the alleged development in Israel's thought from corporate responsibility to individual responsibility. Surely this way of viewing Ezekiel seriously misrepresents the biblical evidence.

But let us accept that some Old Testament material does suggest that one trend in the complex area of thought about responsibility was towards a greater concern for the life of the individual. For example, the book of Job explores the problem of undeserved suffering and seems acutely aware of the enigma of a righteous individual living a life of anguish and distress. The book of Job is almost certainly from the late period of the Old Testament, after the Exile of Judah in Babylonia in the sixth century BC. That same late period saw the development of the belief in personal resurrection, and it is likely that one influence on the growth of this belief was a sense that the lives of particular individuals should at some point receive appropriate reward (or sometimes punishment). Nevertheless, this concern with the individual is just part of the picture in post-exilic Israel, a complex picture which, as we have seen, contained a number of elements which viewed responsibility in more corporate and communal ways. We certainly cannot think of a simple one-way development towards individualism. Sometimes we may even detect shifts in the opposite direction. For example, some scholars have suggested that part of the originality of the great eighth-century prophet Amos was that, unlike some of his predecessors who had condemned particular individuals, he addressed a message of judgement to the nation of Israel as a whole. One further reason why we should be wary of the developmental theory we have been considering is the problem of the difficulty of dating material, an important issue in all biblical studies. As we have seen, a number of passages relating to responsibility in the Old Testament contain both communal and individualistic elements. Even if passages are found which give a straightforward line on responsibility, they would have to be datable to some degree of certainty if they were to lend support to a developmental theory. Such certainty is in fact rarely attainable.

We conclude, then, that the developmental theory relating to ideas about responsibility in Israel should be regarded with great caution, and we suggest that throughout Israel's history the complexities of the relationship between the individual and the group were for the most part recognized as clearly as they are today. The rich variety and complexity of the Old Testament does not lend itself to neat patterns imposed upon it by scholars, and as a general rule one should always be suspicious of such systematizing.

More than once in this discussion we have warned against bold assertions about 'Israelite Thought' and it is appropriate now to look more directly at the question of unity and diversity in Israel, as a theme closely related to the issue of the individual and the community, the one and the many. It is risky to attempt to speak about 'Israelite Thought', either as a distinctive way of thinking or as a set list of beliefs, above all because there was in Israel such a wide variety of ways of thinking and such a broad range of beliefs. In this respect of diversity, ancient Israel was like any other culture. To be sure, as we saw at the start of this chapter, there was a particularly strong sense of national identity in Israel, based primarily not on ethnic or political identity, but rather on shared allegiance to the one God, Yahweh. Perhaps it was the very strength of this religious bond, sometimes described in terms of a covenant, or agreement, between Yahweh and Israel, which allowed there to be, within the broad unity of Israel, such a rich diversity of thought and belief. If we are to appreciate the full richness of this diversity, we should resist the tendency to think of the Old Testament as one book (a tendency encouraged perhaps by the traditional practice of setting the Old Testament apart as sacred Scripture) and view it rather as the library of a nation, reflecting that nation's varied experiences of God over many generations.

It seems that the people who made up the nation of Israel really became conscious of themselves as forming a distinct nation during what we call the period of the Judges. Many scholars believe that the traditions in the Old Testament which speak about the period before that, the traditions of Abraham, Isaac and Jacob, and even perhaps the tradition of the Exodus from Egypt, may well all reflect the experiences of only parts of what later became Israel. It is likely that as the nation of Israel took shape during the period of the Judges, different groups (such as particular tribes), contributed stories about their own past histories to the national pool of tradition and that when the first history of Israel's past came to be written (probably some time in the tenth century BC) these different elements were woven into the story of what was now regarded as the one nation, Israel, bound together by the worship of one God, Yahweh, whose hand was seen in all the many partial histories which now made up Israel's national history.

However, even after the early period, basic differences remained between the parts which made up the people of Israel. The most profound of these differences was that between North and South. In about 922 BC these two areas, which had formed a united monarchy under David and his son Solomon, fell apart when the northern territory broke away and established an independent monarchy. These two Hebrew kingdoms even fought wars with each other and were in many respects very different from one another; certainly as different as, for example, England and Scotland. Many scholars attempt to trace certain parts of the literature of the Old Testament to one or other of the Hebrew kingdoms. For example, the first great historical work of Israel, which is called by scholars the Yahwist Work, and which is to be found in Genesis, Exodus and Numbers, was probably written in the South. On the other hand, most scholars trace the tradition represented in the book of Deuteronomy to the North. A confusing fact to be aware of is that the Northern Kingdom called itself Israel in contrast to the Southern Kingdom which called itself Judah. Confusion can arise because the name Israel was often used to describe the whole People of Yahweh (Northern and Southern), regardless of political divisions. The two kingdoms existed side by side until 721 BC, when the empire of Assyria engulfed the North, exiling many of its inhabitants. A rather similar fate befell the South in 587 BC when the Jerusalem temple was destroyed by Babylon and many southerners were exiled to Babylonia. This created two communities of Judeans, those in Judah and those in Babylonia. Scholars attempt to assign the literature of this exilic period to one of these two communities. For example, the central section of Isaiah, chapters 40—55, often called the work of Second Isaiah, is usually thought to have been composed, for the most part at least, in exile in Babylonia, whereas the Book of Lamentations, for example, is usually regarded as having been written in Judah during the Exile. Such literature is generally seen to reflect the life and concerns of the particular community which produced it, but it must be admitted that it is often very difficult to be at all sure of the place of origin of the literature. Though some southerners returned from Babylonia later, many remained and from this time onwards the widespread geographical diversity of the people of Yahweh further complicates the picture—we speak of the Dispersion of the Jewish people, Egypt being another place to which considerable numbers of southerners moved, especially from the sixth century onwards (see Jer. 43.4–7).

The northerners who were exiled by the Assyrians in 721 BC disappear from view, but we catch occasional glimpses of the remnant of the northern community (e.g. in 2 Chron. 30). Later, we become aware of the existence in the north of the Samaritans, who were increasingly despised by the southern community, which regarded itself as the one true Israel.

In terms of geography alone, then, it may be seen that what we call Israel was an incredibly diverse phenomenon. Moreover, the time-scale covered by the Old Testament is vast. It is really a library produced over a period of about a thousand years. Small wonder that the Old Testament contains such a rich diversity of theology. For example, we find a number of different attitudes to the institution of the monarchy. If one reads 2 Samuel 7 or some of the so-called royal Psalms, such as Psalms 2 and 110, the Davidic monarchy is seen as a primary channel of Yahweh's favour to Israel. However, if one turns to 1 Samuel 8 or 12 or to Deuteronomy 17, monarchy seems to be seen as a rather dangerous threat to the true worship of Yahweh. Another example is provided by Israel's system of sacrificial worship. Large sections of the book of Leviticus, for example, are devoted to detailed legislation for this, but if one turns to the prophets, such as Isaiah or Amos, one finds a vigorous criticism of Israel's complacent reliance on its system of sacrificial worship, which at times seems to come very close to a rejection of the whole system. And so it may be seen that it is virtually impossible to isolate a theological orthodoxy in the Old Testament. Within a community strongly conscious of itself as the one people of Yahweh we nevertheless find a vast range of theological opinion and religious belief and an equally extensive range of ways of expressing these. The Old Testament is the rich deposit of the lively theological tradition of a very diverse nation over many centuries; and it is this which makes it such an exciting subject of study.

To summarize then, we began this chapter by considering the strong emphasis on the importance of the community which characterizes much of the Old Testament. We noted, however, that we today sometimes think in terms of corporate groups as well as in terms of individuals and we argued that it is therefore unreasonable to regard such language as reflecting a 'primitive' mentality when it is found in the Old Testament. Next, we considered the theory that Israelite thought developed smoothly from an emphasis on the corporate responsibility of groups and communities towards an ever-increasing emphasis on the responsibility of the individual. We argued that this theory does not do justice to the evidence of the Old Testament, which suggests rather that at all periods there were some corporate elements and some more individualistic elements in thought about responsibility in Israel. In the final section of the chapter, we suggested that it is moreover impossible to speak of 'Israelite Thought' as something which can be pinned down or described precisely, because Israel was such a diverse entity, extending through many centuries, increasingly spread out in many lands, and producing a great variety of religious literature. We noted the paradox that this rich diversity existed within a nation so strongly conscious of its identity as a community. This tension between diversity and unity may be said to reflect the tension between the individual and the community which we have seen to characterize the Old Testament as a whole. These are tensions which remain very much a part of our modern experience.

NOTES

1   H. W. Robinson, *The Christian Doctrine of Man* (3rd edn Edinburgh, T. & T. Clark, 1926). See especially Robinson's *Corporate Personality in Ancient Israel* (rev. edn Philadelphia, Fortress, 1980).

2   H. W. Robinson, *The Cross in the Old Testament* (London, SCM, 1955), p. 77.

3   J. W. Rogerson, 'The Hebrew Conception of Corporate Personality', *JTS* 21 (1970), pp. 1–16.

4   See Rogerson, *JTS* 21 (1970).

5   For a classical presentation of this position see W. Eichrodt, *Theology of the Old Testament*, vol. ii (London, SCM, 1967; Philadelphia, Westminster, 1967), pp. 231ff.

FOR FURTHER READING

G. E. Mendenhall, 'The Relation of the Individual to Political Society in Ancient Israel', in J. M. Myers *et al.*, ed., *Biblical Studies in Memory of H. C. Alleman* (Locust Valley, J. J. Augustin, 1960), pp. 89–108.

J. R. Porter, 'Legal Aspects of Corporate Personality', *Vetus Testamentum* 15 (1965), pp. 361–80.

6

Old Testament Theology

JOHN BARTON

I

Most Christians would probably say that when they read the Old Testament, they expect (since it is part of the Bible) to learn from it truths about God. They expect it to tell them what he is like, what he has done, and what he requires of them by way of moral conduct. Most Christians who approach the Old Testament in this way, however, are soon disappointed. They find that the God it shows them is, at best, something of a mixed blessing. Although at times he is loving, gentle, and trustworthy, at others he seems capricious, harsh, and unfeeling. The things he is said to have done include not only bestowing miraculous blessings (chiefly on the Israelites), but also destroying whole nations without pity; and the conduct he demands, though it can be recognized as putting a high value on justice, often seems to lack important elements of what we might call Christian love. In short, the information about God we get from the Old Testament seems fairly ambiguous, and we would be hard put to it to say that we recognize in it the God in whom, if we are Christians, we profess to believe.

In one way the kind of critical study of the Old Testament that has been described in the previous chapters alleviates the discomfort. A critical approach shifts the emphasis away from reading the Old Testament to discover what God is like, and on to studying it in order to discover what the ancient Israelites *thought* he was like. Again, instead of learning from its pages what God has done, we learn what the authors or the communities who produced the various Old Testament books *believed* he had done; and by applying historical methods we can sometimes discover what the actual events were that they interpeted as 'acts of God'. In the same way, rather than being able to extract from the Bible a catalogue of moral duties that God lays on us, we try to understand how ideas about ethics developed in ancient Israel, in the course of its history. Because we are now at one remove from the actual assertions the text seems to make about God, the problem of the more 'scandalous' parts of the Old Testament becomes that much less acute. We are not being asked to say that God actually did or said or commanded what the Old Testament says he did: only that people *thought* he had done so. Old Testament study becomes the study of the history of Israelite religion, social life, and institutions. Since this makes no direct claims on our own religious allegiance, we can be much calmer and cooler about it than we could be if we really thought the Old Testament was a source of direct information about God that had to be believed by the Christian, just as it stood.

But on the other hand it takes little effort to see that what is lost here is as much as what is gained. In gaining an objective knowledge of the historical development of religious beliefs in Israel, we seem to have lost the Bible as a book of faith; and the Old Testament has ceased to be a problem by becoming, from the believer's point of view, more or less an irrelevance. The history of the religious beliefs of the ancient Israelites is, no doubt, a very interesting subject for scholars to study, but so are a great many other things, and it is not at all clear why students of *theology*—still less ordinary Christians—should continue to concern themselves with the Old Testament, if this is all it can inform them about. If the Old Testament is to continue to be important for theology, it will have to be on the basis of some way of using it that goes beyond what mere historical criticism can offer; and it is the attempt to provide this that is usually described as 'Old Testament Theology', though, as we shall see, the results of making such an attempt are very varied indeed.

II

There is one possibility for reuniting the Old Testament, studied critically, with Christian theology, that is likely to occur to most people who are at all familiar with the conclusions of biblical scholars. It is a line of interpretation quite often taken in designing school syllabuses in biblical studies, and a convenient shorthand phrase for it would be the 'winding quest' approach. [1] On this way of looking at the Old Testament, it does not (as a non-critical reader might think) give us direct information about God; but by showing us the various stages through which the religious awareness of the Israelite people passed, it enables us to see how they were prepared for the fuller 'revelation' of God brought by Jesus. Thus, even when we have established that the Old Testament is primarily of value in what it can tell us historically about the religious beliefs of Israel, we can still press it directly into the service of theology. We can see it as the record of various attempts to understand God, which were all more or less imperfect, but which nonetheless were necessary and helpful steps on the path that eventually led to Christianity and the theology of the New Testament.

Most often, along these lines, the 'religious quest' of ancient Israel is presented as a *gradual progress* towards the truth. Thus it may be stressed that the blood-thirsty religion and morality of the book of Judges, for example, represents an early stage of religious awareness, and that it was gradually left behind as higher insights into God's nature made themselves known through the teaching of the prophets. The four-source hypothesis of the Pentateuch can be fitted quite well into such a theory of 'progressive revelation'. According to this hypothesis, the sources (J, E, D, and P) derive from three distinct phases within the history of ancient Israel, characterized by different types of religious thought, with J (the earliest source) reflecting an early and very anthropomorphic idea of God and P (the latest) a much more refined, transcendental and monotheistic faith.

But we can go much further in the direction of emphasizing that the quest was a 'winding' one, with many backslidings and false trails, and yet still use the same basic pattern. We can say that the Old Testament bears witness to an enormous variety of religious insights and convictions, many of which strike us as crude or unacceptable, but which were all necessary in paving the way for the emergence of the pure monotheism that lies at the root of both Judaism and Christianity. Without the warlike spirit exemplified in Judges, people would never have come to a really serious awareness of the absolute holiness of God, and of his total and exclusive demands—however wrong they may have been to think that these demands meant actually destroying those who worshipped other gods. Without the ritualistic religion of temple and sacrifice, we should never have come to see the costliness of religious allegiance, nor have appreciated the meaning of vicarious suffering which is so crucial to a Christian understanding of the atonement. And without the prophets, interpreting all the events of history as God's judgement or as his blessing, we should never have arrived at the belief that one God controls the entire course of the world according to principles of both justice and mercy. All these types of Old Testament religion were more or less flawed, but they nevertheless represent essential stages through which human religious awareness had to pass if it was to lead, in the end, to the great religious system of faith in which the modern believer stands.

A number of objections can be raised to this approach, even on the purely historical level. Against the idea of 'progressive revelation', it can be pointed out that many of the ideas of early Israel were by no means dead in New Testament times: for example, the ideal of 'Holy War' as set out in Joshua had enjoyed a considerable resurgence in the second century BC, in the days of the Maccabees. Again, it is easy to think of ways in which Judaism after the Exile seems to have regressed rather than made progress, at least according to our standards. Where the pre-exilic prophets had denounced Israel and threatened that God would destroy his own people for their sin, post-exilic prophecy and apocalyptic writing often confirm the nation in its narrow nationalism and are smugly complacent about God's grace towards it. We have seen that the four-source theory can be fitted into a framework of 'progressive revelation'; but it is interesting to note that Wellhausen, who gave this theory its classic expression, did *not* at all see 'P' as marking an advance on the earlier sources, but as evidence of the decline into narrow legalism and ritualism which were to be condemned by Jesus and St Paul.

Even on the 'winding quest' view, there are many byways of Old Testament faith and practice that it is difficult to argue for as *necessary* preconditions of later Judaism or Christianity. But for our purposes there is a much more fundamental problem. If we are now at the end and goal of the quest, why should we concern ourselves so much with the earlier stages? If it is true that Israel's religious quest leads up to and is fulfilled in the Christian faith, would we not do better to concentrate on the fulfilment than to spend much time on what it fulfilled? It may be true that the Old Testament is mainly of value as showing us how we got to where we now are; but, if it is true, it is not clear that this gives us any better answer than before to the question why anyone concerned with actual religious or theological *truth* should be interested in the Old Testament. The critical method, we suggested, shows us not what God is like, but what people *thought* he was like. If we want to use its findings in theology, it is not at all clear that we shall make any progress by saying, in effect, 'Still, what people in Israel thought God was like bore some likeness to what we now think, and knowing about it helps us to understand how we came to think as we do.' At best, this can be only part of the answer to the question of how the Old Testament, once studied critically, can still be part of, or contribute to, Christian religious belief. After all, it is the Old Testament itself that is part of the Bible, not the reconstructions of the stages in the religious awareness of ancient Israel which we can make from it.

III

It seems, then, that 'Old Testament Theology' will have to be distinguished rather more sharply than this from 'the history of Israelite religious thought', if it is to be useful to us today. Perhaps a hopeful place to start is by noticing two features which one can easily fail to see, when one is engaged on detailed, piecemeal study of the texts.

First, although critical scholars rightly stress the enormous diversity of material within the Old Testament, it is a pity if this leads us to overlook the very obvious *family likeness* between the many texts of which the Old Testament is composed. Certainly, it does not have the inner coherence of a collection of works by a single author; and no doubt there are a few books in it that strike even the superficial reader as swimming against the current, even as contradicting much that is said elsewhere—Ecclesiastes is the most obvious case, but there are others. But we have only to try to imagine how the Old Testament would look to someone brought up in a Far Eastern religious system, such as Hinduism or Taoism, or to see it as it looks to a modern secular humanist, to realize that it is quite unmistakably the product of a single religious tradition with highly characteristic insights and emphases. The very fact that we immediately feel the author of Ecclesiastes is swimming against the current is a sign that there *is* a current, and that we have some idea of the direction in which it flows. Those who adopt the 'winding quest' view are clearly right in thinking that there is a certain unity in the religious thought of ancient Israel, as modern scholarship recon- structs it, even if what they build on this idea is less convincing. The Old Testament may not be one book, but it is very different from a random collection of 'texts from the world's great religions'. We can see that the texts composing it hang together with some coherence as texts. And furthermore, if we try to reconstruct the religious milieu from which these texts came, we are bound to find that it looks like a reasonably unified religious culture. These books plainly do not come from a series of unrelated cultures that practised completely different religions. At one level, and for some purposes, we shall want to insist that all Old Testament books are different— just as we should want to say that all Englishmen are different, and that one ought not to make sweeping generalizations about 'the English mentality'; but, taking a longer view, we shall be bound to concede that it *does* make sense to speak of 'Old Testament religion', just as it makes sense to speak about 'the English' if we are trying to distinguish them from the Americans or the Japanese.

Secondly, beneath the actual assertions that Old Testament books make about what God is like, what he has done, or what he has commanded—which vary a good deal—there are a number of *shared assumptions*, which (again) are perhaps more easily noticed by readers to whom the religion of Israel is rather alien than by those immersed in the study of it. In a sense, this is another way of formulating the point just made, for the family likeness between Old Testament texts owes as much to what they take for granted as to what they positively assert. One of the ways in which a system of belief can be identified is by noticing the points on which its adherents agree even when they are engaged in debate or disagreement with each other. Thus it could be pointed out that even when the prophets stress that God intervenes actively in human affairs (e.g. Amos 8.9–10), whilst Ecclesiastes positively denies that he does so (e.g. Eccles. 1.9), they are working with the shared assumption that God is a being distinct from the world and transcending it, of whom it would at least make sense to say that he had or had not intervened. They are both equally far from a system such as pantheism, in which God simply *is* the world. In such a system, God cannot 'intervene', because he is not distinct from the world. To say he had intervened would be simply meaningless.

So instead of valuing some parts of the Old Testament more highly than others, or following the development of Israelite thought reconstructed as lying behind it (as the 'winding quest' view does), we might try rather to identify its distinctive or characteristic features. This means looking for beliefs held in Israel, and attested in the Old Testament, that explain the *family likeness* which so much of this material shares. In doing this, we should be trying to find the shared assumptions that help to unite such apparently diverse works as the books of the Old Testament; and we might then be able to see how they have managed to function for such a long time as the Scriptures of a coherent religious tradition.

IV

It would be fair to say that most important modern approaches to the problem of formulating an 'Old Testament Theology' have begun from approximately the point of view just outlined. They have rejected the simple distinction with which we began, between the Old Testament as a text, to which Jews and Christians turn for information about God, and the history of Israelite religious belief as reconstructed by critical study of the Old Testament. Rather, they have seen the two as inextricably bound up together. It would, indeed, be strange if the faith which the Old Testament in its finished form brings to expression were wholly different from the beliefs actually held at different periods in ancient Israel; or if the family likeness that these books exhibit rested on a quite different basis from the family likeness that characterized the religion of the ancient Israelites. But actually identifying the basic features that make up the likeness, and the shared assumptions that give it its force, is no easy task. One can often sense the distinctive atmosphere of a corpus of literature, or of an historical period, but it is harder to analyse and state it in a way that will satisfy others who may, nevertheless, be equally convinced that there is indeed something distinctive about it. We might briefly consider the two major attempts at writing a 'Theology of the Old Testament', those of Walter Eichrodt[2] and Gerhard von Rad,[3] and then go on to examine the contribution made by what is called the 'Biblical Theology movement', whose influence is still important in many (especially popular) presentations of the subject.

Eichrodt published his *Theology of the Old Testament* over the years from 1933 to 1939; von Rad's *Old Testament Theology* appeared much more recently, in 1957–60. But they are alike in concentrating on what we have called the *family likeness* of the Old Testament texts at the level of what their writers explicitly *said* about God and Israel and the world, rather than probing into their underlying assumptions. Eichrodt and von Rad both set out to present the *faith of Israel*, the body of beliefs that all who claimed to belong to the people of God in Old Testament times were committed to. This faith united the people of Israel, and it also united all the writers of the Old Testament, who were part of that people.

Both of these scholars organized their presentation of the faith of Israel by taking one particular theme as the clue to the family likeness between the great majority of the Old Testament books— and therefore as likely to have been a dominant theme in the thought of the Israelites over a very long period.

In Eichrodt's *Theology of the Old Testament* the organizing principle is the *covenant* between God and Israel. If we ask what kind of God the ancient Israelites believed in, Eichrodt's answer is that they believed in a covenant-God: that is, a God who had chosen them from among all the nations and entered into a binding agreement with them, which had the character of a contract. God promised to keep his side of the bargain, to continue the blessings which he had begun in his act of choice—a choice which Israel owed purely to his grace, and had done nothing to deserve; whilst Israel, for its part, was under an obligation to maintain the contract by loyalty to God, exclusive worship of him, and obedience to his commands. These commands were summarized in law-codes (especially short digests such as the Ten Commandments), and also communicated from time to time through accredited prophets. It is this basic covenant-pattern which explains the common flavour of very large tracts of the Old Testament; and it was the Israelites' common conviction that God was as such a pattern portrays him that kept the tribes united through their long history, and enabled them (alone among the nations of the ancient Near East) to live on as a religious community even after their national independence had been lost.

Von Rad's organizing principle is a very different one: the theme of *saving history* (or salvation history—in German *Heilsgeschichte*).

For him, the distinctive and characteristic feature both of the literature of the Old Testament and of the religious beliefs of ancient Israel is a conviction that God directs the history of his people, and that he acts on their behalf in accordance with a pattern of saving action established first in leading their ancestors out of Egyptian bondage and giving them the Promised Land as their home. Passages such as Deut. 26.5–9, which von Rad believes to be very ancient, sum up the essential events which provide the key to the God of Israel's manner of acting. It was because they allowed this pattern to serve as a means of interpreting all their experience, that the Israelites were able to give coherence and meaning to the very varied events that befell them in their long history; and it is this same pattern which provides the basic shape of the crucial first six books of the Bible, Genesis–Joshua (often referred to as the 'Hexateuch'). Thus, again, the shape and form of the Old Testament matches the shape of the basic theological convictions of the community from which it derives, and that shape is the shape of the *saving history*: the record of God's acts with and for his people, guiding them and delivering them from their enemies. If we ask what kind of God the Old Testament presupposes, the answer will be: the kind of God who is encountered in the saving history.

It is important to see that in the work of these two scholars, and indeed in most Old Testament theologies, we are not being asked to believe either that the Old Testament speaks with a single and unambiguous voice, or that all ancient Israelites believed identical things. A 'Theology of the Old Testament', as Eichrodt and von Rad understand it, is about the *main stream* of faith in Israel, and in a work as large as the Old Testament any attempt to identify the main stream is likely to run into a certain number of exceptions. But so long as the great bulk of the Old Testament material, and of the experience of Israel as we can reconstruct it, seems to make good sense when read from this particular point of view, the attempt is broadly justified. As a matter of fact, both Eichrodt's and von Rad's theologies, though they have many weaknesses, do enable readers to find their way through the Old Testament material in such a way as to feel its characteristic atmosphere. Although they do repay detailed study, both also lend themselves to being read fairly quickly so as to pick up the main thrust of what is being said. Both, in different ways, present a picture of ancient Israel's faith which owes a lot to the book of Deuteronomy; and a good way to start work on the theology of the Old Testament is to read Deuteronomy, perhaps with a straightforward commentary,[4] in conjunction with either Eichrodt or von Rad.

But do such statements of the 'theology of the Old Testament' help us in our desire to find a use for the Old Testament within theology? They seem, after all, to remain essentially historical statements about the convictions of ancient Israelites, even if they are at a higher level of generality and sophistication than piecemeal studies of the theology of this or that biblical writer, or of the beliefs of this or that historical figure. Both Eichrodt and von Rad claimed, in fact, that their work constituted 'theology' in a more profound sense than this. They were not trying to provide merely descriptive, historical statements of what ancient Israelites 'happened' to believe, leaving aside the question of truth or falsehood; they were trying to show to what kind of God the Old Testament read as a whole, and the whole sweep of theological thought in ancient Israel understood as a whole, bore witness. And they were convinced that this God was congruous with the God witnessed to in the New Testament also, and was indeed the true and living God, no mere creation of 'man's religious quest'. In a sense, then, with these 'theologies', we are back to reading the Old Testament in order to discover the truth about God (or, better, to *encounter* God). So far from a critical approach getting in the way of this, Eichrodt and von Rad in their different ways are suggesting that it is precisely a proper historical-critical study of the text that will indicate the crucial place held by covenant or saving history in the thought of ancient Israel. And then we shall realize that if we read the Old Testament with these interpretative categories, it will prove to be a vehicle through which God is revealed as he truly is. The 'unedifying' parts cease to be a problem (as they remain on most theories of 'progressive revelation'—why should God *ever* have allowed people to think of him as a bloodthirsty warrior?) once they are seen to be time-bound expressions of a perception about God which is in itself *still true*.

Of course the people in the days of the Judges who thought God took pleasure in 'Holy War' and the ruthless destruction of Israel's enemies were mistaken. But this was not because they had a mistaken idea of what God was like: it was because they drew the wrong conclusions from an idea about God which was in itself perfectly true. What they read *out of* their religious belief in a God of covenant-loyalty, or a God who acted in the nation's saving history, was quite wrong, because they had not realized that such a God could not possibly demand violence and blood. But the content of their belief, the actual idea of God's character to which Israel was committed, was and remains true. God really is a God who stands in a relationship of covenant to his people, giving and demanding loyalty; God really is committed to saving his people in their history. So what the Old Testament writers were positively trying to convey—the faith to which they were committed—is still true. What must be abandoned are some of the corollaries of this faith, some of the false conclusions people drew from it. But these do not affect the truth of the faith itself.

For several reasons it is hard to feel completely happy with these approaches. It may be true that people in Israel perceived God in the way Eichrodt or von Rad believed; and it may be true that the way they perceived God is the way God actually is. But even if one or other of these scholars is right in his description of the faith of Israel, it is hard to see how we can be sure that the faith of Israel was right! We would probably want to agree that we are likely to get a more accurate picture of what the Israelites believed from careful scholarly research into Old Testament texts, than we would if we just relied on a naive and superficial reading of them. But even if Eichrodt or von Rad give us a completely satisfactory historical description of what *Israel* believed, that still leaves the question of what we ought *ourselves* to believe wide open. Study of the actual assertions that the Old Testament makes about God, and of the family likeness between them all, seems to have reached the limit of its possibilities in the magisterial works of these two scholars, and it leaves us still unable to give an answer to the question we began with—the question of what we can learn from the Old Testament, not about what people have thought about God, but about what God is actually like. It is time to look at another possible approach.

V

We have just seen that Eichrodt and von Rad, for all their differences, began from what the Old Testament *said explicitly* about God and his relation to Israel, mankind, the created world. There remains, however, the possibility of concentrating more on the shared assumptions *underlying* what the various biblical writers say. This is the area which was the main concern of a number of biblical scholars of the 1950s and early 1960s, whose work has come generally to be known as the 'Biblical Theology Movement'.[5] In many books from this movement, the unity of the Old Testament, indeed of the Bible as a whole, was perceived as being less a matter of all its writers agreeing in what they asserted, and more a feature of their underlying thought-patterns. For example, 'biblical theology' would have agreed with von Rad in placing 'history' at the centre of the Old Testament witness. But von Rad saw 'saving history' as a way in which Israel deliberately gave a shape and pattern to its experience, so that what happened to the Israelites was interpreted through a specific theological tradition as part of God's gracious purposes for their salvation. As we saw, 'saving history', according to him, was part of Israel's faith, something to which Israelites consciously committed themselves. For 'biblical theology', on the other hand, the ancient Israelites simply saw the world in terms of historical movement, and their God was a God whose whole mode of being was historical, whose nature was to be actively involved in human history. It was not that the Israelites had consciously *decided* to believe in such a God; the idea was embedded in their thought processes. It was not that the Old Testament ever *said*: 'Yahweh is a God whose nature is to be involved in history'; rather, this truth was presupposed throughout the Old Testament.

Sometimes scholars from this school of thought went so far as to argue that the distinctively Hebraic way of thinking, underlying the Old Testament, was built into the structures of the Hebrew language. For example, it was sometimes pointed out that the word which we translate as 'truth' in the Old Testament derives from a Hebrew verb which usually has the meaning of 'be firm', 'be steadfast'. From this it was argued that 'truth', for the Israelites, was not a matter of intellectual conviction or objective scientific proof, but of personal commitment and confidence.[6] 'To believe' in the Old Testament would then mean, not to think that some statement is true (to believe *that* . . .), but to commit oneself to something or someone, to put one's trust in something (to believe *in* . . .). Quite often the point was made that there was a great contrast between, on the one hand, Hebrew culture and Hebrew assumptions about reality, which tended to highlight personal commitment and involvement, and on the other hand, western philosophies (deriving ultimately from Greek thought), with their emphasis on intellectual knowledge and objective, rational thought. 'Truth' was one of a number of terms that seemed to fit this distinction; 'love',[7] 'time',[8] and 'body'[9] were others.

'Biblical Theology', then, was a way of understanding the Old Testament and its importance for the Christian reader that looked behind the text, and tried to grasp the basic ideas and categories of thought with which Israel worked. The Christian was supposed to learn how to 'think Hebraically'. This did not mean trying to accept all that the Old Testament asserted about God—for instance, it did not mean believing all the details of the Exodus as the Old Testament describes them. It meant seeing the world in the way Israel saw it, and in that way encountering the God of Israel, who could not be contained in any abstract theological system.

The biblical theology movement itself is now largely dead, but its influence lives on in all sorts of subtle ways. The contrast between Hebrew and Greek modes of thought, and the notion that Christian theology should prefer the former, is still quite widespread; but, more important for our immediate purposes, it is still very commonly suggested that the main function of the Old Testament in theology is as a source of 'concepts', 'ideas', or 'themes'. Biblical studies are sometimes taught, at both school and university level, in terms of 'biblical ways of thinking', and this owes much to the 'biblical theologians'. Sometimes the Old Testament is referred to as a 'resource' from which ideas such as covenant, divine action in history, righteousness, or faith, can be drawn out and used in formulating Christian theology or grounding Christian ethics. In this, again, we see the awareness that it is difficult, in the light of biblical criticism, for the Christian to turn directly to what the Old Testament says as a source of information about the nature or will of God, and a consequent wish to find other ways in which it can nevertheless continue to be fruitful for theology. 'Biblical theology' provided the means of doing this by suggesting that the real focus of revelation or religious truth within the Old Testament lay in the Hebrew mentality to which it bore witness; and it recommended that the modern believer should seek to adjust his own way of thinking so that it, too, functioned in terms of the concepts and categories which constituted that mentality.

Again, however, we may well feel uneasy. Apart from the fact that most Old Testament scholars have largely abandoned the positions taken up by the 'biblical theologians', it is in any case not at all clear why religious truth should be sought at the level of underlying assumptions or concepts rather than at the level of actual conscious belief. One way of putting this is to say that 'biblical theology' helps us to dig in the Old Testament, as in a mine, for styles of thinking or basic concepts which might be useful in constructing a living faith; but once the concepts have been extracted, the texts themselves are discarded like slag. 'Biblical theology' shows us how to *process* the Old Testament text, but not how to *read* it; it sees the theological value of the Old Testament as belonging at the level of an underlying thought-pattern, rather than as lying in the *actual books* of the Old Testament as we now have them.

Besides this tendency to focus on something other than the Old Testament itself, there is in any case a problem in seeing modes of thought or types of concept as the place where religious truth is to be found. In itself, after all, a concept such as 'divine activity' is religiously neutral: what is of interest to the believer is not so much *that* God acts, rather than being passive or 'static', but *how* he acts. It is small comfort to be told that it is God's nature to do things, if we are not told what sorts of things he does. And yet again we are faced with a familiar problem: it is of no use to commend certain categories as 'biblical' or 'Hebrew', or to insist that the 'real' meaning of the Old Testament is to be sought at a level below that of conscious affirmation, when what the ordinary reader of the Old Testament is looking for is theological *truth*. It may be the case that we shall understand the theology of the biblical writers better by grasping the difference between Hebrew mentality and modern thought-modes, but that does not help us to know whether or not the biblical writers were *right*. The Old Testament cannot provide its own validation; we need to know what sort of authority it has, before our improved interpretative tools (if indeed they are such) will take us any further towards using it in the quest for knowledge about—or of—God. 'Biblical theology' is quite defensible in principle as another refinement of historical method, but it is no more of a solution to the problem with which we began than are the Old Testament theologies associated with Eichrodt and von Rad.

VI

Despite these doubts about the value of the 'biblical theology' approach, however, our discussion of it has thrown up one idea which may help us to take the quest for an integration of theology and biblical study a little further. We suggested that one of the features giving Old Testament literature its undeniable flavour of belonging to a single tradition was to be found in the large number of shared assumptions which the various books have in common. 'Biblical theology' tended to identify these assumptions as existing at a very deep, more or less unconscious level—seen in certain aspects of the Hebrew language, in processes of thought beyond the reach of conscious expression, and in ways of looking at or perceiving the world which ancient Israelites could not have articulated even to themselves, so much did they form a part of their mentality. But it is not necessary to go to these lengths in the quest for the distinctive and unifying features of the Old Testament, and of the religious culture of ancient Israel. The Old Testament is held together by a number of generally agreed tenets which are—and were when it was written—perfectly capable of being articulated, but which are in fact very rarely insisted upon in the text, very rarely the point at issue. One of these, so obvious that it almost escapes notice, is the existence of God. Only in a very loose sense could it be said that we 'learn of' God's existence by turning to the Old Testament. There is no passage in the Old Testament which asserts, as a new piece of information, that there is a God. This is not necessarily to say that the men who wrote the Old Testament could not help believing in God, or that the possibility of atheism would have been meaningless to them, as is sometimes asserted. But it does mean that they all take it for granted that their readers will share their conviction that God exists—that the subject is not on the agenda for discussion.

Though it may sound an equally surprising thing to say, it is very difficult to find passages in the Old Testament that are intended to *convey the information* that this God is the creator of the world.[10] For the author of Genesis there does not seem to be the slightest interest in *asserting* that God made the world. One does not get the impression that his readers were in any doubt about this, or needed persuading of it. His purpose is to *recount* the events of creation, and if he is seeking to impart any fresh information, it is almost certainly to be found in the details of the account—the neat division of the work into days, and the fact that the process reaches its climax in the Sabbath—rather than in the mere fact of the world's owing its being to God. That God exists, and is the creator, is a fixed datum for all the biblical writers. In the Old Testament we learn more about a God who is already known, rather than meeting him as if for the first time. The Old Testament writers assume that their readers are familiar with God, and have a reasonably clear picture of his general character. They then proceed to tell them what he has done—or even *how* he has done what he is already known to have done; to praise him for these acts; to comment on human life and behaviour in the light of God's known character; to deal with events and predicaments that seem to call it in question; to remind people of the obligations that they believe him to have laid on them, and to suggest motives and grounds for honouring them; and to predict what he may be expected to do in the future.

If we look at the matter in this way, our initial sense that the task of Old Testament theology is to find some way of bridging the gap between the desire of the scholar for information about what Israel believed, and of the modern believer for information about what God is actually like, seems to reflect a certain misunderstanding about what we can expect to find in the Old Testament. Rather little of the Old Testament is designed to be a source of information, in any narrow sense of that term, in any case. The Old Testament on the whole is the literature of a community that shares a large number of assumptions about God; and many of the theological formulations that we need to make if we are to do it justice are not derived from what it says, but are *summaries of what readers must already* know if they are to understand it. Very few parts of the Old Testament consist of 'doctrine' or direct 'teaching' about God. Indeed, the only books that are unequivocally presented as teaching, the so-called 'wisdom' books of Proverbs and Ecclesiastes, are generally agreed to lie somewhat off the main line of Old Testament thought; and in any case they are explicitly presented as *human* teaching rather than as the utterances of God.

VII

What, then, is the goal of Old Testament theology as a branch of biblical study? As with all other biblical study, we should think of it not so much as a matter of extracting information from the Old Testament, or of summarizing its theological content—which are the essential models we have been considering up to now—but more as providing explanations that will help us to read and use the Old Testament with more understanding. The Old Testament is not primarily a source of *information*, either about God or about people's ideas of God; it is primarily a collection of various kinds of *literature* whose main themes and subject-matter are religious. And with literature, which in this respect is very different from a text-book or a catechism, one cannot extract the 'message' and then discard the wrappings; the 'message' is inextricably bound up with the way in which it is presented. The role of Old Testament theology is to help us to understand this particular collection of literature by explaining the various concepts it uses, the kind of God it presupposes, the ways in which its authors thought this God had acted, and what they believed he had commanded. Its role is thus nearer to the role of (say) a guide to the Elizabethan thought-world in helping us to understand Shakespeare, than it is to the function of a handbook of Christian doctrine. There should be no thought in our minds that the author of a 'Theology of the Old Testament' tells us what the Old Testament *really* says more clearly than the text itself. His job is the purely ancillary one of helping us to understand the categories and ideas with which the Old Testament text works. As in the case of Shakespeare, so here: no reading of critical literature can be a substitute for actually reading the Old Testament text for ourselves; and when we do read it, it is not in order to 'extract' information from it, but to come, through it, to grasp the realities of which its authors speak.

Thus, for example, an 'Old Testament Theology' can help us to understand what idea of God is presupposed by the Psalms, and can list the attributes that the psalmists saw him as possessing: power, glory, uniqueness, transcendence, mercy, and so on. It can make these ideas much more precise than would ever be possible on a simple reading of the text, and can fill them out by showing how they are dealt with in other parts of the Old Testament, and how they differ from modern ideas that may seem superficially similar. But a psalm itself is not correctly seen as designed to 'teach' us these things, for a psalm is a text which the worshipping community sings *to* God, not any kind of communication addressed to the worshipper, either by God or by anyone else. The only proper way to 'use' a psalm, in the end, is to sing it, not to study it as a possible source of information. Similar things might be said about the narrative texts which make up much more than half of the Old Testament. Studies of the theological beliefs of ancient Israel will help us to read them with understanding; but they were not written to provide information about these theological beliefs, they were written in order to tell a story or recount a history. In this sense the 'theology' of the historical books is a secondary concern; although God figures in the stories, and they do not make sense except on the basis of various beliefs about him, they are not designed to tell the reader things about God, but rather to narrate events from a particular point of view. We discover what their authors are trying to say by reading their account, not by abstracting the theology embedded in it and discarding the framework.

The practical effect of these suggestions is to make rather more than is made in the Old Testament theologies discussed so far of the distinction between the Old Testament text, on the one hand, and the life and culture of ancient Israel which constitute its background, on the other. We saw that it will hardly make sense to distinguish them in such a way that the Old Testament is read in a sort of vacuum: obviously, it must be read against its background, and the beliefs of those who produced it will be those of the society in which they lived. Much recent Old Testament study has rightly stressed that most books in the Old Testament were in any case not produced by 'authors' in our sense at all, but are the crystallization of the thinking of the community at large. But we still ought to keep in mind that there is a distinction to be made between the Old Testament text and those who wrote it, on the one hand, and the great mass of ancient Israelites, on the other. Important though it is to be aware of the context of ancient Israelite life and belief against which Old Testament books make sense, it is equally important to remember that they may not be merely an expression of beliefs held very commonly or very widely in Israel. The Old Testament, is, in effect, the 'official' version of ancient Israel's life and thought, the *classic* formulations of the community's faith that it chose to hand on to future generations. The task of elucidating the background of religious belief that enables us to make sense of this text is therefore not the same as the task of expounding the text itself. We have suggested that the Old Testament theologian can be usefully employed in the first of these tasks—and the second part of this book will be given over to 'Old Testament theology' in this sense. But the second task, the exposition of the text itself, is (like all exposition of texts) not a matter of the expositor's constructing his own system, but of enabling the reader to hear the text itself. On this level biblical scholarship does not provide raw materials for systematic theologians to use, by extracting the 'theology' from the Old Testament text for them; rather, it enables the systematic theologian (or the Christian believer) to hear more clearly what the text is saying, and to construct this theology, or practise his faith, as someone to whom the Bible has been enabled to communicate its own message in its own way.

VIII

So there are really two purposes which a book called 'The Theology of the Old Testament' could usefully serve. One is to provide us with all sorts of background information which will help us to understand the religious tradition within which the Old Testament writings belong. Because these texts come from a rather remote culture, we need expert help in understanding the shared assumptions with which they work and in terms of which they make sense. As a matter of fact, it is at this level that Eichrodt's *Theology* actually functions best, even though it claims to do something rather different: it reconstructs the religious thought of the ancient Israelites (for which, of course, the Old Testament provides the great bulk of evidence) and thereby prepares us to read the text with more understanding. Another way in which we can approach the matter is by trying to analyse the actual theological statements made in various Old Testament books, and also to find ways of describing the theological atmosphere or implications even of those that are not primarily written to convey 'teaching'. Then we can go on to synthesize the results (if it proves that the family likeness among the various books is strong enough to justify it), so as to produce a summary of the theological impression that a careful reading of the whole Old Testament is likely to make. This comes nearer to what von Rad was attempting. Either way of writing an 'Old Testament Theology' is likely to be useful to the student, and both seem to be legitimate approaches. Our discussion has suggested a few pitfalls, however, and we may conclude by saying a little about them.

First, the distinction between the two kinds of project needs to be kept clear, even if in practice we want to say that the results of each are congruent with those of the other. A description of the religious beliefs of Israel in different periods is not the same as an analysis of the leading themes or topics of the Old Testament, and there is no direct line from one to the other. Both Eichrodt's and von Rad's works—and this is also true of books produced under the influence of 'biblical theology'—tend to suffer from a failure to be clear which of these two things they are talking about. As we have seen, both are needed, but they need to be kept distinct.

Secondly, we need to know whether we are seeking to describe what was believed in Israel or stated in the Old Testament, on the one hand, or to say what is in fact the case, as a matter of theological truth, on the other. Again, the Christian at any rate will believe that there is some correlation between the two, though different people will have different ideas about how close the correlation is. If we have any sort of doctrine of scriptural inspiration, it must include a belief that it is somehow providential that we have the Scriptures we do, that God wants us to understand him by means of these particular texts; and that must also entail that the existence of various shared assumptions and beliefs in ancient Israel, which were necessary if those texts were to be possible, was also in some sense intended by God. But this is essentially separate from the purely empirical questions of what people in fact believed, or what the text actually says. Our answer to the first question must not be allowed to colour our reconstruction of Old Testament theology, in either of the senses just discussed, so as (for example) to make us see this as a gradual development from worse to better ideas of God, if the actual evidence does not point in this direction. In fact, the discussion of the last section suggested that the type of material the Old Testament contains is in any case not ideally suited to analysis in terms of the 'idea of God' it is trying to convey. It functions much more obliquely than that, by telling stories, singing praises, and speaking in aphorisms about life; and if it is to be fruitful for modern theologians and believers (as any doctrine of inspiration insists that it is), then this will be more because these people listen to what it is actually saying, in the way it chooses to say it, than because they can reconstruct from it the beliefs of its authors or the religious experiences of the community that lies behind them. At any rate a modern interest in 'using' the Old Testament in Christian theology must not be allowed to influence our understanding of what it says, in its own right; and our desire to overcome the problem with which we began must not lead us to fudge the evidence on the historical level.

Thirdly, nothing is gained by exaggerating the unity either of the Old Testament or of the religious assumptions and beliefs of ancient Israelites. As we saw, neither Eichrodt nor von Rad was trying to claim that the Old Testament spoke with an absolutely single voice, though the 'biblical theology' movement did tend very much in this direction. But any synthesizing work on Old Testament theology is apt to blow up the admitted family likeness of the material into a virtual identity of content, and to speak as though there were beliefs held by 'Israel' as such which remained absolutely constant throughout the 'Old Testament period'. Against this it is certainly right to say that the Old Testament contains a variety of theologies, and attests a variety of religious perceptions and convictions, varying with period, with social group, even perhaps with geographical location. It is perfectly reasonable to look for unifying themes and common features which account for the fact that this is manifestly the literature of a single broad tradition. But sometimes Old Testament scholars first locate what seems to them the 'centre' of the Old Testament, or of the religion of Israel, and then reject certain parts of the text as 'not truly Israelite'—the very frequent treatment of the wisdom books as uncharacteristic of Israelite thought is the most striking case of this. When Old Testament theology is written in this way, it ceases to be descriptive of what is actually the case and starts to issue directives about what ought to be the case. Often we find that strains of theological thought are being described as 'central' to the Old Testament because they chime in best with a particular scholar's own ideas of theological truth. When this happens, the discipline of Old Testament theology ceases to serve the reader and becomes his master, forcing him to read the text from a standpoint artificially imposed upon it. It is to be feared that even the great *Theologies* are sometimes guilty of this, and there is no doubt that the kind of material contained in introductory books, especially when these are arranged thematically, very often has this effect. The only remedy against it is for students to insist on actually reading the text for themselves and not to accept any generalizations about its central themes or insights which they cannot find evidence for in their own reading.

NOTES

1   *Winding Quest* is the title of an excellent abridged Old Testament for children by A. T. Dale (London, Oxford University, 1972; Wilton, Morehouse-Barlow, 1973). It does not put forward the approach I am describing here—its title simply provides a useful phrase.

2   W. Eichrodt, *Theology of the Old Testament* (London, SCM, 1967; Philadelphia, Westminster, 1967).

3   G. von Rad, *Old Testament Theology* (Edinburgh, Oliver & Boyd, 1962–5; New York, Harper & Row, 1962–5).

4   For example, A. Phillips, *Deuteronomy*, Cambridge Bible Commentary on the New English Bible (Cambridge, Cambridge University, 1974).

5   On 'biblical theology' see especially B. S. Childs, *Biblical Theology in Crisis* (Philadelphia, Westminster, 1970). Some important books from this period which give a fair picture of the general themes of 'biblical theology' are:
A. T. Richardson, ed., *A Theological Wordbook of the Bible* (London, SCM, 1950; New York, Macmillan, 1951).
G. E. Wright, *God Who Acts* (London, SCM, 1958; Chicago, H. Regnery, 1952).
N. H. Snaith, *The Distinctive Ideas of the Old Testament* (London, Epworth, 1944; New York, Schocken, 1964).
G. A. F. Knight, *A Christian Theology of the Old Testament* (London, SCM, 1959; Richmond, John Knox, 1959).

6   See the discussion of this approach in J. Barr, *The Semantics of Biblical Language* (Oxford, Oxford University, 1961), pp. 161–205.

7   See, for example, A. Nygren, *Agape and Eros* (London, SPCK, 1957; New York, Harper & Row, 1969).

8   See O. Cullmann, *Christ and Time* (London, SCM, 1957; Philadelphia, Westminster, 1964).

9   See J. A. T. Robinson, *The Body. A Study in Pauline Theology* (London, SCM, 1952; Philadelphia, Westminster, 1977).

10   This may sound rather surprising. For a long time it has been common for critical scholars, when attacking fundamentalist ideas about the 'verbal inerrancy' of Genesis 1—2, to argue that what these chapters are 'really about' is not the details of the creation, but the *fact that* God is the creator. Some fundamentalists have now begun to say the same. After all, if the real meaning of the passage is that God made the world, rather than that he made it in six days and according to the detailed blueprint provided in Genesis 1, then the passage is inerrant after all.

The actual inaccuracies of the details need not undermine the general fundamentalist position, if once it can be argued that the only thing the author was positively trying to assert was that God is the creator. In point of fact, it seems clear that the author was really very interested in the details—and therefore, in fundamentalist terms, was actually mistaken—while taking for granted the fact that God was the creator.

FOR FURTHER READING

R. E. Clements, *Old Testament Theology: A fresh Approach* (London, Marshall, Morgan & Scott, 1978; Atlanta, John Knox, 1980).

R. B. Laurin, ed., *Contemporary Old Testament Theologians* (Valley Forge, Judson, 1970; London, Marshall, Morgan & Scott, 1972).

J. W. Rogerson, 'Progressive Revelation: Its History and its Value as a key to Old Testament Interpretation' in *Epworth Review*, 9 (1982) pp. 73–86.

D. G. Spriggs, *Two Old Testament Theologies*, Studies in Biblical Theology, Second Series 30 (London, SCM, 1974; Geneva Ala., Allenson, 1975).

7

Approaches to Ethics in the Old Testament

JOHN BARTON

I

> Then Samuel said, 'Bring here to me Agag the king of the Amalekites.'
> And Agag came to him cheerfully. Agag said, 'Surely the bitterness of
> death is past.' And Samuel said, 'As your sword has made women
> childless, so shall your mother be childless among women.' And Samuel
> hewed Agag in pieces before the LORD in Gilgal.   (1 Samuel 15.32-3
> RSV)

This passage perfectly epitomizes, in many people's minds, the
ethics of the Old Testament. A bloodthirsty God exacts vengeance,
and will not be moved by entreaty; the agents of God must close
their hearts to any natural human pity. This is the kind of thing that
people have in mind when they say that someone has 'an Old
Testament attitude' to morality. Yet, on the other hand, it is also
from the Old Testament that we have what is often regarded as a
perfect summary of Christian moral conduct:

> What does the LORD require of you but to do justice, and to love
> kindness, and to walk humbly with your God? (Micah 6.8)

And it is, after all, in the Old Testament that the 'two great
commandments' of the law, love for God and for one's neighbour,
are to be found (Deuteronomy 6.5 and Leviticus 19.18), whatever
apparent dross they may be mixed in with. An initial dip into the
ethical ideas of the Old Testament might suggest, then, that they are
merely chaotic. It is hardly surprising that there are so few books on
Old Testament ethics, if the Old Testament material swings so
wildly between extremes. Perhaps, we may feel, the Old Testament
has no really coherent message on this subject.

One of the purposes of this chapter will indeed be to suggest that the Old Testament enshrines a great variety of ethical points of view, and that there is no more one 'ethics of the Old Testament' than there is one 'theology of the Old Testament'. Nevertheless, in the later sections of the chapter we shall go on to suggest that the picture is not one of total chaos, but that certain clear lines may be discerned. Before we can present either side of the case properly, however, we need to make it much clearer what is meant by the rather vague phrase 'Old Testament ethics'.

II

'Old Testament ethics' can refer to two related but distinct things. Sometimes the study of 'Old Testament ethics' means the study of the historical development of ideas about morality, or of actual moral conduct, in ancient Israel. In this sense, to study the ethics of the Old Testament is like studying the ethics of medieval Europe, or classical Greece, or modern China. Such a study is not necessarily 'merely' historical. As we saw when discussing the study of religious belief in ancient Israel, Christians are likely to believe that ancient Israelites were in certain important ways in touch with God, so that what they thought about moral obligation is of more than purely antiquarian interest to us. Nevertheless, it *is* historical, primarily: it is a matter of reconstructing, on the basis of the evidence provided by the Old Testament text, and any other evidence that may be available, how people in ancient Israel behaved, and how they thought one was supposed to behave. Such a study yields some very interesting results, which are the despair of anyone trying to reconstruct the ethical 'system' of ancient Israel; for they are very diverse, and suggest that ancient Israelite society was richly varied in its attitudes and practices.

But the second thing we might be doing in studying 'Old Testament ethics' is to take the Old Testament essentially as a book that forms part of Christian Scripture, and to ask what, in its finished form, it has to say to us about ethical issues. As we noted in chapter 6, despite its great variety there is also a strong family likeness about the Old Testament in all its parts. It represents, not just a random sample or cross-section of the beliefs of ancient Israelites, but a sort of official version of these beliefs—an orthodox presentation of Israelite religion and ethics as Israel, in the last centuries before Christ, wished these to be understood. And at this level it does provide a reasonably unified and clear ethical system, though it has to be admitted that this is of such a very high degree of generality that it would be hard for us to apply it in practice in resolving any particular ethical dilemma: it is more a matter of a common flavour or atmosphere, a certain style of approach to moral questions. But if we are studying Old Testament ethics in this second sense there is far less need to be pessimistic about our chances of having something coherent and unified to show for our labours.

The fatal mistake is not to be clear in one's mind which of these two types of enquiry one is engaged in. Quite often discussions of what 'the Old Testament teaches' on a particular moral question do not make this necessary distinction, and shift uneasily between historical questions about whether (say) the Patriarchs recognized or observed certain moral rules, or what the prophets thought Israelites of their day ought to do, and questions about what God is telling us through the Old Testament that *we* ought to do. Of course there may be routes that will take us from one to the other. Any Christian who is persuaded that the Old Testament, as part of the Bible, is in some sense inspired by God, will be committed to believing that there are such routes; but it is merely muddled thinking not to see that the questions are distinct. The Old Testament as a finished book, on the one hand, and the multiplicity of ancient Israelites about whom it informs us in various ways, on the other, are not at all the same thing, and little progress can be made so long as they are confused. It might be helpful to describe the two areas that will need discussion as 'Ethics in ancient Israel' and 'The Ethics of the Old Testament'. In what follows we shall examine each separately.

III

Ethics in ancient Israel

Any historical study of ethical conduct, norms, and systems in ancient Israel is bound to be highly complex, for the Old Testament provides material from which to reconstruct the life and thought of a whole nation over a period of about a thousand years; and we could hardly expect that everything would have remained the same throughout this period, or that the various different social groups within the nation would necessarily have agreed among themselves even within one part of it. Even a cursory examination shows that there is a great variety reflected even within the limited material that actually found its way into the Old Testament, and we can only guess at the much greater bulk of material from which this was selected. By way of illustration, we shall examine three questions in the realm of ethics, on all of which the Old Testament contains indications that there were many different opinions and traditions in Israel. These are (a) actual moral norms; (b) the basis of ethics; and (c) the motives and incentives for moral conduct.

1 Moral norms

It is fairly obvious to any careful reader of the Old Testament that the accepted norms of conduct in ancient Israel varied a good deal. To put it more precisely, we may say that the sorts of conduct people thought to be right can only be described if we take into account at least two variable factors. One of these, obviously enough, is *time*. There are a number of areas of moral concern where we almost certainly have to reckon with change and development from century to century in the long history of Israel. The Old Testament never formally repudiates polygamy, but monogamy certainly became the more usual arrangement in Israel in later times—exactly when, we do not know. Many customs which, it seems, had been comparatively unimportant or even non-existent in the period before the Babylonian exile of the sixth century BC, moved into the centre of ethical interest in the post-exilic age. Among these may be mentioned sabbath-observance, circumcision, and the rigorous keeping of the food laws. All these are 'markers' of Judaism which, though they were probably practised at least by some before the Exile, had not then been a matter of active commitment, because at that time there was an Israelite state (organized on political rather than narrowly religious lines) to maintain the distinction between Israelite and non-Israelite. Some norms of ethical conduct come and go in such a way that one cannot easily speak of development, still less progress, but only of variation. For example, the belief that Israel had a moral duty to wipe out pagans who worshipped other gods, and who tried to seduce or coerce Israelites into doing the same, flourishes in some periods, but seems to be almost forgotten in others. It does not seem ever to have been 'officially' repudiated, but in times of security and peace we do not hear of its being put into action. Some scholars think that in Deuteronomy, where it is quite prominent (see Deuteronomy 12.29–31; 13.1–18), it is to be understood chiefly as a call to total allegiance to Yahweh rather than as a literal command to kill those who worship gods other than Yahweh. Whatever may have been the intention of Deuteronomy, it is clear that such laws were a dead letter for much of the time as an actual incentive to action. In some ways the period from about 200 BC down to the age of the New Testament saw more of a resurgence of this idea than many of the previous centuries, and in a curious way the age of the Maccabees reaches back across the years to touch the period of the Judges (at least as that is reported in the Old Testament). Other parts of the moral code, by contrast, seem to have remained fairly static, and this is true of many areas of conduct where Israel shared in a general ethical tradition common to much of the ancient Near East. Such might be a number of the issues dealt with in the Ten Commandments—murder, theft, adultery; though the way in which the community dealt with breaches of such norms may well have varied from time to time.

Less obvious, perhaps, but arguably even more important, is the variable of *social group*. Comparatively little can be said with confidence about the sociology of ancient Israel: though we can speak loosely of 'tribes', 'families', and 'clans', and of social stratification in terms of 'rulers', 'administrators', 'scribes', of 'priests', 'prophets', and 'wise men', we have only quite rough-and-ready standards by which to distinguish and describe these various groups. Nevertheless even from an Old Testament that has plainly been edited to express the attitudes of the official religious leadership in the post-exilic age, and to smooth out the evidence of dissenting voices, it is clear that in many periods there were sharp divisions of emphasis, and even straightforward disagreements, between different groups in Israel over a good many ethical issues. The pre-exilic prophets consistently speak as though the ethical norms to which they are trying to recall the nation are despised or rejected by those who lead the nation. See, for example, Isaiah 1.15–17; 5.8–23; Jeremiah 7.5–15; 22.1–19; Amos 6.1–7. If the leaders of the nation modelled their lives more on the patterns provided in books such as Proverbs than on the lines suggested by the prophets, it is not surprising that there seems to have been little common ground. As in our discussion of 'Old Testament theology', so here, we must be careful not to ignore the very clear family likeness even between groups as opposed as prophets and rulers appear sometimes to have been; but the differences also are real enough to deter us from speaking of 'the Israelite ethic', as though they represented merely minor variations on an identical theme. In a much later period, as we know from studies of New Testament background, Judaism had many sects and religious groups of very diverse character; and though it makes sense to call them all 'Jewish', since all evinced a basic adherence to the law, the focus of their moral concern varied very widely. We can speak of the ethics of the Qumran community, or of the Pharisees, or of the high-priestly party.

One of the problems in trying to produce a *history* of ethics in Israel (which has, in fact, very rarely been attempted) is that in most periods we do not have evidence for more than a few of the various social strata that made up 'Israel', and often our evidence is for different groups in different periods. One can easily imagine how difficult it would be to write a history of ethics in England if our evidence for the seventeenth century was entirely composed of the writings of philosophers, for the eighteenth of records of parliamentary debates, for the nineteenth of popular novels, and for the twentieth of school reports. Yet something not too unlike this is the situation that confronts us in the Old Testament. It is all too easy to speak, for example, of the post-exilic age as a time of 'increasing legalism', on the strength of the books of Ezra and Nehemiah and material in the Pentateuch, especially Leviticus, which probably reached its final form during or after the Exile. But the fact is that we have, in these books, evidence of what the priests were teaching in the early post-exilic period, and little evidence of what other groups then believed; whereas, for the pre-exilic age, we have a great deal of prophetic material, but hardly anything that we can confidently ascribe to priestly circles. For all we know they may have been just as 'legalistic' before the Exile as after it: there is simply no evidence one way or the other. So far, then, as actual moral norms recognized in Israel are concerned, we can perfectly well speak of some general tendencies, so long as we stay at a fairly non-specific level; but when we come down to details, the material at our disposal dissolves into a fascinatingly varied, but quite unsystematic jumble.

2 The basis of ethics

Ancient Israel possessed nothing that could be described as 'moral philosophy', no attempt to work out systematically the basis on which ethics rests, and to clarify why it is that moral imperatives or norms have the binding character that people attribute to them. In this sense, the Old Testament is not speculative or philosophical literature. Nevertheless, it does make sense to ask what in ancient Israel was thought or felt (perhaps at a fairly inarticulate level) to be the underlying basis of morality. The short answer most readers of the Old Testament would give to this question is 'God', and this would certainly be right, for most of the thinking that is attested in the Old Testament. There is, it is true, a certain amount of evidence within the Old Testament that some Israelites thought in terms of merely human *conventions* in certain areas of morality, rather than of divine authority: much of the so-called 'wisdom' literature, such as Proverbs, has this character, and expressions such as, 'Such things are not done in Israel' (2 Samuel 13.12), may point in the same direction. Furthermore, most people no doubt gave little thought to the question whether morality derived from God or not! But by and large the Old Testament registers only religious attitudes to morality, and it shows that, at least for those who produced it, God was very much at the centre of ethical obligation.

To say this, however, is not to say all that can be said about the basis of ethics in Israel, for morality can be religious in more than one way. Perhaps the simplest form of religious morality is found where people think that ethics is a matter of doing what God tells them. Either they devise ways of discovering what God's will is (through oracles or prophets or accredited teachers such as priests); or else they interpret laws and precepts that are actually in force as expressions of the will of God, and claim that they have been revealed at some specific time. (Perhaps this is currently so; we are not concerned here either to support or rule out this possibility.) The Old Testament contains plenty of material that shows such a view to have been common in Israel at many periods. Some such model is obviously present in the story of Moses receiving the law on Sinai (Exodus 19–23), and in accounts of people asking priests or prophets to rule on difficult questions of morality (see Haggai 2.10–19); and the idea of the covenant, as a book like Deuteronomy presents it, is that Israel must perform the obligations which God lays on it as the terms of his contract with the nation.

On the other hand, the wisdom literature, as we see it in Proverbs, looks at morality in a rather different way even when it does try to relate it to God. Here we find fewer references to God as the giver of laws or moral norms, and more interest in presenting morality as a matter of fitting one's life to the orders and patterns observable in the world which is God's creation. This has some affinities with what the western tradition of moral philosophy has usually called 'natural law'. There is a good example of this way of thinking in the book of Job (31.13–15), where Job acknowledges that he has a duty to act justly towards his slaves because they, like him, were made by the same God and therefore share the same nature. This is very different from the idea that we find repeatedly in Deuteronomy, where the Israelites have an obligation to be kind to slaves because God *commands* them to be, as part of their side of the covenant relationship with him. Indeed, this example brings out another way in which Israelite writers sometimes seek to express the basis of human morality; for Deuteronomy also argues that the Israelites should be kind to slaves because *God* is kind to them, as is proved by the fact that he took pity on their own forebears when they were slaves in Egypt—see Deut. 15.15. Here an appeal is being made to what we might call the 'imitation of God' as the foundation of ethics, an idea that Martin Buber[1] argued was fundamental to the Old Testament, though there are not in fact many passages where we can be confident that it occurs. Even when it does, it does not necessarily mean that a very exalted or sublime kind of morality is being commended. After all, the quotation with which this chapter began was in a sense concerned with the imitation of God! If God is seen as one who exacts bloody retribution, then the idea that ethics is the imitation of God may well lead to an 'inhuman' standard of morality. On the other hand, insights into morality may come to be reflected back onto the understanding of God himself, so that people come to say: *We* must not exact vengeance, but rather show forgiveness; how then can we believe *God* to be less merciful than we know we ought to be ourselves? There is a discussion of this sort of reasoning below, on pp. 128–9. We can say, then, that there are at least three models or 'theories' of God's role in relation to human moral obligation which the Old Testament shows to have been current in ancient Israel: obedience to God's commandments, conformity to the patterns and orders of the world, and imitation of God's own character and conduct. These can, indeed, be merged in various ways, as we shall see; but at least we seem to be justified in saying that on the question of the basis of ethics, as in the area of particular moral norms, the Old Testament bears witness to a rich and varied world of thought. In recommending various courses of action as morally right, the people who produced the literature of the Old Testament were able to draw on a number of different approaches and these, presumably, found some echo in the minds of the Israelites to whom their work was addressed. Once again, then, we seem to need quite a pluralistic presentation if we are to do justice to ethics in ancient Israel.

3   *Motives and incentives to moral conduct*

Much the same needs to be said of another area that interests students of ethics: the question of sticks and carrots, of incentives to act well and threats of the consequences of acting badly. What did people in Israel think would happen to them if they behaved wrongly; what motives did they have for behaving rightly? Here we shall naturally be concerned mostly with the evidence provided by those books that seek to admonish or instruct the readers, especially the so-called 'law books' of the Pentateuch; and in these we find once more a rich variety of approaches—particularly well discussed in Eichrodt's *Theology of the Old Testament*. vol. ii, chapter 22.

One might classify the incentives to moral conduct in the Old Testament very roughly by saying that some look to the future, some to the past, and some to the present. Incentives are, in our way of thinking, most often a matter of holding out some promise of future reward or threat of future punishment, and this kind of incentive is certainly very plentiful in the Old Testament too. The Ten Commandments contain one such: 'Honour your father and your mother, that your days may be long in the land.' The early collection of law generally known as the 'Book of the Covenant' or 'Covenant Code' (Exodus 21—23) has another: 'If you take your neighbour's garment in pledge, you shall restore it to him before the sun goes down ... for if he cries to me, I will hear, for I am compassionate' (Exodus 22.25–7)—a barely-veiled threat to the would-be offender. The wisdom books, of course, also abound in such incentives—indeed, it might be said that one of their major concerns is to urge that righteousness brings prosperity and unrighteousness disaster, even to the point where commonsense is outraged.

But there is also often an appeal to the past, to the gratitude to God for what he has done that ought to prompt one to obey him or to order one's life in the right way. Deuteronomy is particularly rich in passages stressing this aspect of the matter: 'Your fathers went down to Egypt seventy persons, and now the LORD your God has made you as the stars of heaven for multitude; you shall therefore love the LORD your God, and keep his charge, his statutes and ordinances,' (Deuteronomy 10.22—11.1). It also occurs, as we have already noted, in the injunction to be kind to slaves out of gratitude for God's kindness to Israel's ancestors when *they* were slaves; and in the Deuteronomic version of the fourth commandment: 'Observe the sabbath day, to keep it holy . . . that your manservant and your maidservant may rest as well as you. You shall remember that you were a servant in the land of Egypt, and the LORD your God brought you out thence with a mighty hand and an outstretched arm . . .' (Deuteronomy 5.12–14).

Though it is perhaps slightly forced to speak of an incentive based on the *present*, one might describe in this way some of the Old Testament passages that insist on the inherent moral beauty of God's laws as reason enough for keeping them: the law itself is a treasure which the Israelite possesses by observing it, and what more could anyone ask? Psalm 119 is probably the best exposition of such a view in the Old Testament: 'I opened my mouth, and drew in my breath for joy, for my delight was in thy commandments' (Psalm 119.131). But Deuteronomy, again, thinks along these lines: 'What great nation is there that has statutes and ordinances so righteous as all this law which I set before you this day?' (Deuteronomy 4.8). The suggestion that the law is to be kept because it is inherently good—the kind of law that anyone in his senses would be only too pleased to have a chance of keeping—greatly stresses the goodness and reasonableness of the God who gives such a law. God is not an arbitrary tyrant, but knows what is best for his people; and this in itself is an incentive to do as he commands.

The Old Testament, therefore, and still more the life of Israel that lies behind the Old Testament, presents an enormously rich and varied range of attitudes towards ethics in its various aspects. Ethics in ancient Israel is a neglected subject, but one that deserves a great deal of attention.

IV

The ethics of the Old Testament

In discussing Old Testament theology in chapter 6 we saw that, when all allowances have been made for the diversity of actual theological assertions within the Old Testament, and of religious beliefs in the society from which it derives, it still makes sense to ask about the overall character of the theological tradition which the finished work enshrines. The same is true for ethics. Before the rise of historical criticism, readers of the Old Testament were far less aware than we are now of the diversity of the material it contained; but this is far from meaning that they did not notice problems in reconciling one part with another, and in extracting any clear and consistent moral teaching from it. Yet, on the whole, they thought that the Scriptures of the Old Testament had a 'general drift', which made it possible, with care, to see them as broadly supporting some ethical positions and ruling out others; and this is far from being a foolish or unreasonable approach to adopt. Our best course will be to go back to two of the areas we examined under the heading of 'Ethics in Ancient Israel', and see how they look when approached from the angle of the Old Testament as a finished work, as part of Christian Scripture. We shall deal with (a) moral norms and (b) the basis of morality.

1 Moral norms

The problem that we immediately face when we try to discover what actual moral principles or norms can be extracted from the Old Testament text is that the Old Testament text does not seem designed as a mine from which these things are meant to be extracted. Although it has long been customary for Christians to understand the Old Testament as 'law'[2] (taken to mean something like 'regulations for living'), such an approach immediately faces the problem that rather little of the Old Testament's contents actually have the *form* of law. As we saw, very large parts of it are composed of narrative, hymnody, or prophecy, and the texts in which positive instructions are issued as to how people ought to live make up only a tiny fraction of the whole. Even though the Pentateuch is traditionally called 'the Law' (we shall examine this in the next section), this is clearly in a somewhat extended sense of the term, for even Leviticus and Deuteronomy, which contain primarily 'legal' or 'instructional' material, are given a narrative framework; while Genesis and Numbers are almost exclusively narrative, and contain scarcely anything that we would naturally call 'law' at all. Both Judaism and Christianity have in the past developed complex systems of interpretative method that would enable them to extract 'law' in the straightforward sense ('rules') from this heterogeneous collection of material. But, as with 'theology', it can be argued that it is false to the nature of the material to see it primarily as a quarry from which 'ethics' must be dug by whatever tools can be devised for the purpose. If it is to inform our ethical judgements, we might rather say, this will be because we allow our understanding of what it is saying *on its own terms* to work on our minds, as we face the issues on which we ourselves must make our own ethical decisions.

This certainly means that the quest for 'proof texts' will not serve our purpose, and this of course is true for any use of the Old Testament that seeks to take critical study seriously. But, in any case, on most of the ethical questions the Old Testament deals with about which we are likely to be in any doubt, a proof text approach is of no use, since the evidence is conflicting. Texts can be assembled both in favour of and against polygamy, capital punishment, divorce, and war. Notoriously, on one issue which is very hotly debated among Christians today, one can cite directly conflicting judgements from Old Testament Scripture. This is the question whether armed resistance to lawfully constituted authority is justified in the name of ethical or religious principles. This issue clearly arises in the case of the bloody coup instigated by Elisha and accomplished by Jehu (2 Kings 9—10). The author of Kings applauds this as a work of loyalty to God; Hosea (1.4) condemns it utterly, and pronounces God's imminent vengeance for it. Once we resort to proof texts, all the diversity with which the previous section dealt becomes a source of confusion and despair.

But this masks the general problem of how we are to evaluate ethical ideas contained in material of such diverse *character*. Neither Kings nor Hosea, after all, is couched in the form of *law* or even of moral teaching: Kings is narrative, with occasional commentary inserted into it, and Hosea is prophecy, delivered for the occasion and not necessarily generalizable, as it would need to be if we were to build an ethical system on it.

To make any progress in the face of this difficulty we shall have to stand back a little further from the detail of the Old Testament, and make rather more of the 'general drift' idea just mentioned in connection with older interpretations. Although it is quite true that very much of the Old Testament does not have the form of law, the principle that was at work in the process leading to its becoming 'Scripture', and being understood as in some way a single work, was certainly that the reader should be able to derive profit, both religious and moral, from reading it in *all* its parts—not just those that directly address him with words of prohibition or command. And as a matter of fact most of the narratives do, either directly or incidentally, tend to establish some sorts of moral value as commendable and others as unacceptable; and the prophetic books, and even the Psalms, though they do not lay down moral norms in the manner of a lawcode, can only be appreciated, or assented to, or used liturgically, on the assumption of a broad general agreement with and adherence to a moral tradition which (though it may not be easy to define) does have some distinctive content. For example: even if we did not have the laws (in Deuteronomy and elsewhere) actually forbidding certain types of orgiastic religious rites, it would be clear from reading the historical books that the 'official' theology which these books present, as part of the canon of Scripture, is against such things. Although we may not be able to point to any particular text and say that it forbids such rites in a way that is plainly binding on the modern believer—we cannot appeal to passages in the histories as 'proof texts'—it is difficult to think that one could ascribe *any* kind of authority to the Old Testament and still think that this was compatible with a religious practice that included orgies. It would immediately strike anyone who actually practised a religion that did include this element, that the Old Testament, taken in its general drift, has an ethos into which it does not fit! To say, as we must, that there is enormous variety in the Old Testament, that on some important issues it is deeply ambiguous, that much of it is not directly concerned with inculcating ethical attitudes anyway—all this is true; but it remains the case that the Old Testament can only make coherent sense within a particular religious and ethical system, which can be specified and described, even if only in very general terms.

Even when there is real disagreement within the Old Testament—as on the question of whether the pagan world stands under God's judgement, and should be rejected and even physically attacked (compare I Samuel 15 with Jonah)—we can sometimes see that the disagreement takes place against a background of certain common assumptions. I Samuel and Jonah both assume that Yahweh is a God who demands total allegiance and whose purposes must not be resisted by man, even though the practical conclusions they draw from this are plainly opposed, and there is no point in our pretending otherwise. A Hindu might well be struck by the fact that both works assume that it is a matter of the highest importance to worship the right God and to seek to discover his will, neither of which might figure prominently in his scheme of things. Because we are nearer to the Israelite-Jewish ethical tradition ourselves, we are struck by the (undoubted) differences, rather than by the under-lying similarities.

To get the balance right, then, we need to say something like this. Once the Old Testament is read critically, it is difficult to claim it as an unequivocal support for one type of Christian or Jewish ethics rather than another. We are almost bound to concede that it cannot be made to justify the whole system of medieval church law, or to show the way with complete clarity on debated issues of the present day such as abortion or contraception. But this does not mean that it is compatible with *just any* ethical system, that one could take the Old Testament into one's system and at the same time adopt a Hindu or Shintoistic ethical code, or commit oneself to a life of complete hedonism. It is not at all easy to spell out what moral principles are compatible or incompatible with the general drift of the Old Testament, but it is not impossible, at least in principle. Our sense that the moral stance of the Old Testament is simply chaotic derives largely from the fact that it is so much a part of our common western heritage that we cannot stand far enough away to recognize the family likeness among its writings, and thus to see how markedly they differ, as a whole, from those of other major religious and ethical systems. And, if we are biblical critics, our very detailed study of the Old Testament will make us acutely aware of differences within it which, seen from outside, are actually comparatively minor. It is important to keep a sense of proportion.

Of course it remains true that the moral principles on which the Old Testament books are agreed are of a fairly high order of generality—indeed, mostly commonplaces for anyone brought up in traditional western morality. In many cases they are shared with the other Semitic religious systems of ancient and modern times. But a commonplace is not necessarily a banality, especially when we live in a society whose hold on the traditional moral system of the West is no longer so firm as it once was, and where rival views of ethics have become genuine options. It can still make sense, in such a context, to speak of 'the biblical tradition' on particular moral issues, however careful and scrupulous we need to be in recognizing variations within it.

2   The basis of ethics

If we turn, finally, to the question of the basis of ethics, the idea of a general drift in the Old Testament can once again come to our help. In section III it was suggested, with merely a few of many possible examples, how varied the approaches to ethics were in ancient Israel: not even wholly non-religious, 'conventionalist' types of ethics can be excluded, and within the religious tradition of morality there are a number of different threads. But as it stands in its finished form, the Old Testament undoubtedly sees God as the fountainhead of ethical obligation, as of everything else. It is not just, however, that the idea of ethics as straightforwardly 'obedience to God's commands' takes over from all the other ways in which God's relation to moral obligation is understood, but rather that the final form of the Old Testament represents a subtle synthesis of a number of ways of understanding this obedience. The basic category for ethics in the Old Testament is, indeed, 'law'; but 'law' as a translation of the Hebrew *torah*, which is a term of much wider application than 'law' in the sense it normally bears in English. When the whole Pentateuch or, as often in Jewish writings, the whole Old Testament is referred to as 'the Torah', what is meant is an ethical system which includes not only the idea that human moral obligations derive from God as the law-giver, but also the notions which we have designated for short 'natural law' and 'imitation of God'.

The best way to approach the Old Testament ethical system as 'Torah', is to remember that the purpose of the Old Testament is not primarily to give information about morality—any more than it is to give information about theology, as we saw in chapter 6—but to provide materials which, when pondered and absorbed into the mind, will suggest the pattern or shape of a way of life lived in the presence of God. Though the Old Testament *contains* 'laws' or 'rules' in our sense, it contains much else besides, and it cannot simply be equated with a set of rules. Readers are meant to be directed in obeying God's will and living in fellowship with him, not only by carrying out the detailed prescriptions of the laws (in the narrower sense), but also by reading the narratives—which, we suggested, do presuppose and help to establish a pattern of moral behaviour; by worshipping God with the help of the Psalms; and by meditating on sayings of sages and prophets. Thus, for the final form of the Old Testament, practical moral conduct is inextricably linked with what we would probably call 'spirituality': it is a matter of a style of life, not just of particular rulings on 'moral issues'. *'Torah' is a system by which to live the whole of life in the presence of God, rather than a set of detailed regulations to cover every individual situation in which a moral ruling might be called for.* Though this idea can, and sometimes did, lead to a minute attention to details of conduct such as Christians call 'legalism', the motive force behind it was a desire to bring the whole of life under the control of God's rule—to 'accept the yoke of the Kingdom of heaven', as rabbinic sources sometimes put it.

Now the reason why 'Torah' was able to develop this all-pervasive character has something to do with a fusion of the various approaches to the basis of ethics we discussed above. Torah is, first, the legislation delivered to Israel through Moses on Mount Sinai. But if we look at it more closely, we get a clear impression that this is not simply a matter of potentially arbitrary commandments which God gave simply because he chose to. Rather the law affords an insight into the contours of God's own ideal will for his people and for all mankind. This was sometimes expressed in later Judaism by saying that this same law which Moses received existed already before the creation of the world, and served as the pattern or even as the tool which God used when he made the world. As the pattern of

God's mind, the guiding principle of his own conduct as well as of the conduct of Israel, it is rather more like what we might call 'natural law' in many ways. God has made the world in such a way that it exhibits a moral order; and this has the corollary, which was drawn explicitly in later Judaism, but which is already essentially present in the Old Testament, that God himself is in some sense bound by his own laws. Within the Old Testament this conviction comes out most clearly, not in the law-codes themselves, but in those texts that are concerned with what in modern theology is called 'theodicy'. By this is meant books which seek to vindicate the justice and goodness of God, in the face of experiences or arguments that seem to call it in question. The historical books, and many of the prophets, work with a basic conviction which they try to urge on their hearers or readers, that God is just *even on human terms*—that he himself adheres to the same moral principles that he expects mankind to observe, that he is as just as they would like to believe he is. The discussion of Ezekiel 18 (see chapter 5 above) has shown that God is there portrayed as having the same rules for himself and his own conduct as he has for judging the conduct of Israel: contrary to what the exiled community supposed, he cannot be accused of changing the rules to suit himself. Thus 'natural' and 'revealed' law are regarded as one and the same thing; but this is not a matter of mere theory or of definition, it is a conclusion won through a hard struggle with the facts of the nation's experience, a struggle which is duly recorded by the Old Testament writers.

But this fusion of the first two types of approach to the basis of ethics has the effect of establishing the third of them. To do good, on such a view, is to imitate God, to do the things he would do, if he were a human being; and what these things are can be read off in some measure from the things he *has* done, especially his acts of love and faithfulness towards Israel in the crucial early years of her existence—in the Exodus, the giving of the promised land, the establishment of the temple and the other sacred institutions. It is just for this reason that it is essential to record these events. The rules which God requires Israel to observe can be seen to be congruent with his own character only if the events which show what that character is are also recounted. His purposes for the future, in which that character will continue to be consistently manifested, also need to be included in any full account of the basis of Torah; and so the historical books run off without a break into prophetic books which confirm for the reader that God will continue to be in the future as he has been in the past, true to the sorts of moral principle that he lays upon men. It might be said, then, that for the Old Testament as we have it ethics is a matter of imitating the pattern of God's own actions, in salvation and in creation, because these spring from a pattern which always exists in his own mind and by which he governs the world with justice and mercy. Torah—in one aspect simply the law of Moses—is in another aspect the design according to which the world was created, and which makes sense of it; and by adhering to it human beings form part of God's plan, and enjoy a kind of fellowship with him. Though he is transcendent and so beyond human grasp, he is nonetheless knowable, because he shares a kinship with man, and especially with Israelite man; for those who observe Torah are, in a sense, the most fully human people, fully realizing the purpose for which they were made. In this sense ethics is not so much a system of obligations as a way of communion with God, which is a cause for joy: hence the lyrical quality, so puzzling to us who use 'law' in a much narrower sense, of such passages in praise of the law as Psalm 19 or Ecclesiasticus 24.23ff. And hence the existence of the text which has so often struck Christian readers as artificial, repetitive, and legalistic, but which could well serve as a complete statement in miniature of Old Testament ethics and, indeed, of much Old Testament theology—Psalm 119: one hundred and seventy-six verses in praise of the Torah.

NOTES

1   M. Buber, *Kampf um Israel* (Berlin, 1933), pp. 68ff. In English: 'Imitatio Dei', in *Mamre: Essays in Religion* London, Oxford University, 1946; Westport, Greenwood, 1970).

2   See A. J. Gunneweg, *Understanding the Old Testament* (London, SCM, 1978; Philadelphia, Westminster, 1978), chapter 4.

FOR FURTHER READING

J. Barton, 'Understanding Old Testament Ethics', *Journal for the Study of the Old Testament* 9, (1978), pp. 44–64.
H. McKeating, 'Sanctions against Adultery in Ancient Israelite Society, with some Reflections on Methodology in the Study of Old Testament Ethics', *Journal for the Study of the Old Testament* 11 (1979), pp. 57–72.

8

The Old Testament and its Relationship to the New Testament

PAUL JOYCE

How does the New Testament fit into the picture of the study of the Old Testament which the chapters of this book have presented? This is a very natural question, especially since the Old and New Testaments are nearly always found bound together as one book— or perhaps we should rather say that in Christian practice they are usually found together; this is a significant qualification, for it is important to realize that the question of the relationship between the Old and New Testaments is essentially a Christian issue. The very name 'Old Testament', used to define the Hebrew Scriptures, was coined by Christians to distinguish these writings from the literature of the early Church which began to be regarded as having authority. The relationship between these two bodies of literature may well interest the Jew or the historian of religions, but it is within the Christian tradition that the relationship between the two has been a burning issue. In fact the question of what Christians should do with the texts they had inherited from the ancient Israelites was the subject of lively debate from the earliest centuries of the Church.

We begin by reviewing the factors which have often raised problems for Christians when considering the place they should give to the Hebrew Scriptures. One factor has always been the sheer difficulty of the Old Testament. So much seemed obscure and irrelevant. What was to be made of detailed rituals for sacrificial worship, or of long lists of names? How could one explain the glaring inconsistencies within many Old Testament narratives (for example, David is introduced into Saul's court in 1 Sam. 16 as a man of war, but in the next chapter he is a peasant lad, unknown to Saul, who has never worn armour)? And what of the broader theological differences found within the Old Testament (for example, between the generous openness to the nations of the world found in chapters 40—55 of Isaiah and the apparent very narrow nationalism of Ezra)? Another factor which affected attitudes to the Old Testament within the Church was the very Jewishness of the Hebrew Scriptures. What relevance could these texts, produced by the ancient Israelites, possibly have for a Church which had broken away from its Jewish moorings? In the period of the early Church, one person in particular, named Marcion, argued for a total break with the Church's roots in Judaism, and in fact he rejected the old Testament altogether. In the present century, in Nazi Germany, anti-Jewish feeling put pressure upon the Church to deny the authority of the Old Testament. A further factor leading some to question the continued authority and relevance of the Old Testament is the belief that the findings of modern science have contradicted the scientific views represented in the Old Testament and especially in the early chapters of Genesis.

We shall return to these questions, but we now turn to what is arguably the most important factor of all in the difficulties Christians experience when considering the place they should give to the Old Testament, the existence of inconsistencies between the Old Testament and the New. The factors mentioned above all relate to general difficulties about the Old Testament itself, but this factor is more crucial, involving as it does apparent conflict between the Testaments. Let us look at some examples. The alleged cruelty of parts of the Old Testament has caused difficulty to many. A notorious case comes from Psalm 137, which begins with the words, 'By the waters of Babylon . . .'. In the final verse, the Psalmist says to Babylon, the nation which had exiled many of the people of Judah,

Happy shall he be who takes your little ones and dashes them against the rock!

How can this be squared with Jesus' saying in the Sermon on the Mount, 'If anyone strikes you on the right cheek, turn to him the other also'? Such difficulties occur not only with regard to human attitudes and behaviour but also with regard to the picture presented of God. In 2 Samuel 6, we read of poor Uzzah, who touched the ark of the covenant to prevent it falling over as it was being carried to Jerusalem. Uzzah was only trying to be helpful, but he was struck dead by God for daring to touch the sacred object. Such incidents are not common in the Old Testament, but how does the God who appears in them relate to the loving God whom the New Testament encourages Christians to call 'Abba'? Marcion, whom we mentioned earlier, took these questions so seriously that he actually claimed that the loving God of the New Testament was in fact a different God from the angry God of the Old Testament! This may be a rather extreme response, but the problem is one that still worries many today.

Another contrast which has often been drawn between the Old Testament and the New relates quite closely to this. One of the central features of Paul's theology is his assertion that the law of the Old Testament, which Israel was called upon to obey as the people of God, has been replaced in the gospel of Christ by the free gift of grace, or unmerited favour, given to all who believe in Christ. Much of Paul's language tends to stress the contrast between law and gospel rather strongly, but he was also aware of the important place of the Old Testament in the Church. However, some other theologians, since Paul's time, have stressed the contrast between law and gospel to such an extent that they have tended to set up a black and white dichotomy between the Old Testament and the New, with the Old Testament representing a religion of oppression and legalism from which the New Testament frees us. Not surprisingly, on such a view, the continued place of the Old Testament as respected Scripture within the Church often tends to be seriously questioned.

These, then, are some of the major factors which have raised problems for Christians when considering the place they should give to the Hebrew Scriptures. Let us now briefly look at some typical responses to these difficulties. These responses fall into two basic groups, namely those responses which involve rejection of the Old Testament and those which affirm the importance of the Old Testament for the Church.

The classic case of rejection of the Old Testament within the Christian tradition is that of Marcion, about whom we should now say a little more. He was a very influential churchman of the second century, one of those who emphasized Paul's contrast between Old Testament law and New Testament gospel to an extreme degree, so much so that he rejected the Old Testament, which he regarded as speaking of a God other than the God who was Father of Jesus. This clearly placed him outside the ranks of orthodox Christians. The main factors in leading Marcion to reject the Old Testament seem to have been primarily, the problem of inconsistencies between the Testaments, focusing especially on the apparently cruel aspects of the Old Testament, and, secondarily (though for Marcion closely related to this primary factor), the very Jewishness of the Old Testament. However, a significant fact to note at this point is that, in attempting to exclude the apparently cruel and the Jewish elements from the Bible, Marcion was unable to rest content with rejecting the Old Testament. He also had to reject, as secondary additions, large sections of the New Testament where he found similar features.

Marcion's rejection of the Old Testament was deliberate and was part and parcel of his elaborate theological system. The form which rejection of the Old Testament takes today is generally very different, amounting usually to an embarrassed silence about that part of the Bible. This attitude, which might well be said to be typical of very many Christians, is rarely articulated clearly, but seems to derive from a number of the factors we mentioned earlier. Of particular importance here seem to be the supposed difficulty and obscurity of so much of the Old Testament; the apparent cruelty and primitive nature of large parts of it; and also the feeling that the Old Testament is irrelevant to the modern world and even contradicts the scientific views of the modern world.

The alternative to rejecting or quietly ignoring the Old Testament is to affirm its importance for the Church and to attempt to integrate it with one's understanding of the New Testament. This more positive response may take a wide range of forms. A common way of handling the Old Testament in the early Church was to allegorize it. This approach recognized the difficulties presented by the Old Testament and sought to counter them by claiming that the real meaning of the Old Testament was other than the plain sense of the text. For example, the Song of Songs, which is probably secular love poetry, was interpreted as referring to the relationship between Christ and his bride, the Church; or again, the apparently vindictive and cruel parts of a number of the Psalms (for example, Psalm 63, verses 9–10) were often understood to refer to the sinful tendencies within us—it was against these sinful tendencies and not against real human enemies that this violent language was directed. It cannot be denied that such methods often produced a very rich and edifying reading of the biblical text, but nevertheless it is hard to be satisfied with an interpretation of the Old Testament which fails to face up to the plain sense of the text and there are few today who would support this allegorical approach as being the best way to understand the Old Testament.

Much more common in the Church today is what is often called the fundamentalist approach to the Bible. Like the allegorical approach, it attributes a high degree of authority to the Old Testament, but differs in that it generally involves reading the biblical text in a very literal way. It is not unfair to say that, for the most part, this approach tends to ignore the difficulties we considered at the start of this chapter. Inconsistencies are generally harmonized, the differences between various parts or within certain sections of the Old Testament are played down or explained as far as possible, and what cannot be explained is taken on trust as divinely inspired. The harsh elements of the picture of God's activity in the Old Testament are taken very seriously and this often results in a Christian theology in which the aspect of divine judgement looms large. The scientific views of the reader are generally made to conform to what are supposed to be the scientific truths of the biblical text, or alternatively, an attempt is made, however tortuously, to read the biblical text in a way which fits modern scientific theories. Particularly in the United States, dispensational theories (see chapter 1, p. 23) solve some of the difficulties by claiming that parts of the OT refer only to God's purposes for the Jews, and have nothing to do with the Church.

There is no intention here to mock the fundamentalist position. It is sincerely held by large numbers of Christians in the world today. However, it will be suggested in this chapter that there can be no satisfactory way of reading the Old Testament from a Christian standpoint unless the issues considered at the start of the chapter are at least taken seriously as issues. We shall suggest that those problems are by no means insuperable obstacles to a positive reading of the Old Testament, and that intellectual honesty demands that they be at least recognized and confronted.

An approach which faces up to these questions head on, and which yet provides the means whereby the Old Testament with all its riches may be accorded a positive place within the Church would seem to be what is needed. Let us consider how such an approach

ꞏmignt tackle the problems which we considered at the start of the chapter.

The early chapters of the present book introduced the reader to the basic tools of Old Testament study, namely, literary and historical criticism. The use of the word 'criticism' here should not cause anxiety. The word is not used in its negative sense, suggesting an approach which picks holes in the Bible; the word 'criticism' refers rather to the application of rational thought to the understanding of the biblical texts, asking questions about the various literary forms which they take, and seeing them against their historical backgrounds. We noted earlier that the sheer difficulty and apparent obscurity of much of the Old Testament has often been an important factor in threatening the place of the Old Testament in the Church. Literary and historical criticism have shed a vast amount of light on these problems. For example, various inconsistencies or repetitions have in many cases been explained in terms of there being several different literary strands present. For example, the inconsistencies in the story of David's introduction to Saul have usually been explained in this way. Legislation for sacrifice and lists of family descent have become easier to understand when seen against their historical background in the life of Israel, as this has been illuminated by careful study of the biblical texts and the literature of neighbouring cultures. Divergent attitudes, for example, to the place of non-Jews in God's plan, begin to make sense when seen as representing the perspectives of different periods and different groups within Israel. Furthermore, this approach to the Old Testament tends to understand passages such as those in Genesis about the creation of the world and of mankind to have been written for literary and theological purposes, attempting to express the relationship between God, the world and mankind. They need not be seen as scientific texts advancing rival views to those of modern science. It should not be thought for a moment that all the problems presented by the Old Testament have been solved; far from it—many questions remain unanswered and scholars differ in their views about many issues. Nevertheless, a great deal has been discovered; thanks to the application of literary and historical criticism, the Old Testament is no longer a closed book and its alleged obscurity need no longer be an obstacle to its having a positive place in the Church. Moreover, the clarification of much of the obscurity of the Old Testament has removed what was the major taking-off point for the allegorical approach. When sense can be made of the text as it stands, there is no need for elaborate allegory.

However, even where we feel we understand the Old Testament better now, there are times when we are acutely aware of differences and inconsistencies between the Old Testament and the New. We suggested earlier that this is really the crucial issue in the debate over the place of the Old Testament in the Church. What are we to make of Psalms which seem cruel and vindictive? Is not the harsh legalism of the Old Testament incompatible with the gospel of love and grace which we find in the New Testament? A way forward here has too been provided by the application of literary and historical criticism to the biblical texts. We have learned to recognize within both Old and New Testaments a rich diversity of theological standpoints, and this has shown that it is quite inappropriate to think in terms of a sharp dichotomy or absolute contrast between the two Testaments. It is not true that the whole of the Old Testament is cruel and vindictive; nor is it true that the New Testament is entirely without material which can seem harsh, rigorous, even primitive. Let us consider some examples.

It is certainly true that the last verse of Psalm 137 hopes to see Babylonian children dashed against the rocks, but it would be wrong to think of such a violent attitude as typical of the whole Old Testament. In Leviticus 19.18 we read the familiar words, 'You shall love your neighbour as yourself'. In verses 33–4 of the same chapter, this command is extended to enjoin similar behaviour towards any stranger resident among the Israelites. Furthermore, on a still broader scale, there is a strong universalist tradition running through the Old Testament, found for example in chapters 40—55 of Isaiah and in the books of Jonah and Ruth, a tradition which seems to look to the incorporation of foreign nations into the saving plans of the God of Israel. Turning to the New Testament, it is of course true that love and forgiveness are the predominant themes, but we cannot overlook the element of rigorous judgement, as described, for example, in chapter 25 of Matthew's Gospel. In the parable of the Talents, the servant who failed to make good use of the money entrusted to him by his master is cast into 'the outer darkness, where men weep and gnash their teeth'. A few verses later, in a description of the final judgement, the wicked are told, 'Depart from me, you cursed, into eternal fire'. Thus, the Old

Testament does not have a monopoly on such stern language. Such language may be difficult for us to relate to today, but if this is so, it is a problem presented by the New Testament as well as the Old.

We shall have to return to this issue, but first let us consider a further implication of recognizing the rich diversity of both Testaments. We mentioned earlier the tendency in some Christian theology to draw a strong contrast between, on the one hand, the Old Testament emphasis on law and on obedience as the condition of divine favour and, on the other hand, the New Testament gospel of free and undeserved grace, with divine favour being bestowed independently of any demand. Such a dichotomy is, however, quite unjustified, because both Old and New Testaments each contain much material stressing God's demands on his people and also much material stressing his forgiveness and his undeserved favour towards his people. For example, within the Old Testament, there is certainly a good deal of emphasis on the need for obedience to God's law and on the penalties which will follow sin; but there is also material such as that found in Ezekiel 36.26–7, where God promises to give Israel a new heart and a new spirit and so enable Israel to respond to him. Again, in Jeremiah 31.31–4, God promises to write his law on Israel's heart so that she will obey it and assures her that her sin and iniquity will be forgiven. When we turn to the New Testament, Paul's emphasis on God's favour as free grace dependent on no human action is certainly very important, but the diversity of the New Testament also finds room for the Epistle of James, which stresses the need for faith to be expressed in good deeds. There can be then no absolute dichotomy between Old Testament law and New Testament gospel. The tension between demand and grace is vital to both Testaments. The distinctive feature of the New Testament is rather that these themes are related to the person and work of Jesus Christ; just how this distinctive feature of the New Testament relates to the Old Testament is a question to which we shall return shortly.

We have suggested, then, that the Old Testament does not have a monopoly on language which may strike us as harsh, rigorous, even occasionally primitive. We have argued that both Old and New Testaments contain a broad range of theology and language, which in both cases includes at times that which may seem to us stern and difficult. And so we have concluded that there can, as far as these issues are concerned, be no black and white contrast between the

Old Testament and the New, on the basis of which the place of the Old Testament in the Christian Bible might be denied or at least seriously questioned. However, whilst we may have demonstrated that the major problems often raised with regard to the Old Testament apply also to the New, we have not escaped these problems, which are now seen to be relevant to the Bible as a whole. What do we make of the harsh and rigorous language which we find in both Testaments? And how can we account for the presence in both Testaments of a variety of theological viewpoints?

The key to progress in understanding these problems lies in a clarification of what we mean by the authority of the Bible. In what sense is the Bible valid and true? It seems that we need a way of understanding the authority of the Bible which can find room for a rich diversity in the biblical witness, a diversity which can include (even, we suggest, in the New Testament) elements which we may regard as relatively primitive. We should not imagine that the only way of viewing the authority of the Bible is one which assumes that texts must be either absolutely authoritative, in the sense of being timelessly infallible, or else completely without authority. Nor should we assume that the whole of the Bible (or the whole of each Testament) must, if regarded as authoritative at all, be thought of as being uniformly authoritative, with every part being as important or permanently valid as the next.

Both the Old Testament and the New Testament are firmly rooted in history—this is part of their strength. Each was produced in a whole range of cultural settings, addressing the issues of those settings, being influenced by or reacting against the ideas of those times. In this process, literature was produced which reflects the encounter of God with his people, and this encounter is often reflected so profoundly (in the Old Testament as well as the New) that today, many centuries later, much of this literature confronts us with great power. The biblical literature gains much of its authenticity and relevance to our times from its very rootedness in the real world of affairs in which it took shape. However, this very rootedness in culture means that the Bible cannot be regarded as authoritative in an absolute sense which fails to recognize its historically conditioned nature. Nor can it be regarded as authoritative in a uniform way; because the biblical literature inevitably took shape amid the swirling mass of events and ideas which make up human history, it will at different points reflect the encounter of

God with his people with varying degrees of profundity and insight. Moreover, since our own cultural setting is so different from the various settings in which the Bible was formed, it is not surprising that certain parts of the biblical witness will prove helpful to us, or 'ring bells' for us, more than others.

There will be parts of both Old and New Testaments which we shall not find very edifying or relevant, parts which seem particularly tied to the narrow concerns of their own day; for example, the vindictive ending of Psalm 137 or, perhaps, some of Paul's remarks about women or slaves. We would be foolish, however, for this reason to reject the whole of the Bible, with its wealth of profound religious truth, simply because the authority we ascribe to it cannot be an absolute or uniform authority. On the understanding of the authority of the Bible which we are proposing, a diversity in the biblical witness (including at times elements which seem to us relatively harsh) is quite acceptable. And once we recognize this diversity in both Testaments, there can no longer be a black and white dichotomy between the Old and New Testaments. The Old Testament, like the New, is valued and treasured for the riches it contains.

We have seen a number of ways in which the application of literary and historical criticism has clarified and eased some of the problems associated with the relationship between the Old and New Testaments. But if literary and historical criticism have eased many problems in this area, they have, in a sense, raised another. Careful study of the biblical texts by these methods has made very clear the important differences which often exist between the original meaning of certain Old Testament material and the re-use of that same material in the New Testament. We must now address this question of the use of the Old Testament in the New Testament.

The New Testament uses Old Testament material in a wide variety of ways, but we shall here consider just a few characteristic examples. Sometimes it is stated very explicitly that the Old Testament is being quoted so as to show that the events recorded in the New Testament fulfil the promises of the Old. So, for example, we often find in Matthew's Gospel the formula, 'This happened to fulfil that which was spoken by the prophet . . .'. Some cases of the use of such a formula seem to relate Old Testament words to New Testament events in a very profound way. For example, at Matthew

2.15 the words of Hosea 11.1, 'Out of Egypt have I called my son', are quoted in connection with the sojourn of Jesus' family in Egypt. The words are used in Hosea of Israel coming out of Egypt in the Exodus and the parallel with Jesus as representative of the new Israel is pleasing and profound. Some other cases of the use of this formula in Matthew are, however, less satisfying. At Matthew 1.22–3 the words of Isaiah 7.14 are quoted in connection with the virgin birth of Jesus. Unfortunately, in the original Hebrew of Isaiah 7.14 the reference is to the birth of a significant child to a young woman; there is no reference to a virgin birth. It is possible, however, to understand the Greek translation of Isaiah 7.14 to refer to a virgin birth and it seems to be this which Matthew had in mind. We cannot help but feel less than fully convinced by such a case of 'fulfilment' which rests on the wording of a translation rather than on that of the original Hebrew of the Old Testament.

In some other cases, the notion that the events of the New Testament fulfil the words of the Old is implicit rather than explicit. However, such cases are very similar to the more explicit formula we have just considered; they too look at the Old Testament through Christian eyes, drawing freely on Old Testament material to illuminate such questions as that of the status of Christ. Thus, for example, in Mark 12.35–7, Jesus is portrayed as quoting Psalm 110.1 in his debate with the scribes over whether it is appropriate to speak of the Christ (or the Messiah) as the Son of David. Jesus says that in Psalm 110, David, the author of the Psalm, uses the phrase 'my Lord' when speaking of the Christ. Therefore the Christ must be greater than David and so the phrase Son of David is inadequate to describe the Christ. This is a good example of the way that the application of literary and historical criticism to the Old Testament has shown us how far the New Testament understanding of material can diverge from its probable original meaning in the Old Testament. It is now generally accepted that the Psalms were, for the most part, pieces composed for use in the liturgy of the temple. This particular Psalm is usually thought to be from the ceremony of a royal coronation. It would probably be a temple official who would say the words, 'The Lord [that is, God] says to my Lord [that is, the new king of the line of David], "Sit at my right hand"'. The way the Psalm is understood in the New Testament is very different from this. 'My Lord' is understood to refer not to an ordinary Davidic king but to the Christ. This in itself is not an altogether in-

appropriate extension of the meaning of the Psalm, for the hoped-
for Christ or Messiah was to be a great king of the Davidic line.
However, the whole point of Jesus' argument as represented in
Mark's Gospel (that David called the Christ 'my Lord') depends on
David having written this Psalm, whereas Old Testament scholars
are almost unanimous in the view that he very probably did not.

The problem which confronts us is this. How should we respond
to such cases in which the New Testament seems to understand the
Old in ways which do not seem to have been intended by the original
authors? To begin with, we must recognize that many such cases do
exist. Although we cannot by any means always be absolutely sure
that we know what the original authors had in mind, it is a fact that
literary and historical criticism have enabled us in large part to
discern where New Testament use of material diverges from the
probable original meaning in the Old Testament. The New
Testament generally attempts to make sense for its own day of the
words of the Old Testament; this inevitably leads to divergences,
because the backgrounds and concerns of the Old and New
Testaments are so very different. In contrast to the practice of the
New Testament authors, biblical scholars today make a deliberate
attempt to discover, however incompletely this must be, what sense
the Old Testament was intended to make for its own day. We must
have the courage to acknowledge the differences between Old
Testament intention and New Testament understanding, where
such exist; nothing is to be gained from artificial attempts to
harmonize differences of this kind. The Old Testament must be
allowed to be itself; it is not merely resource material for Christian
theology; it is not simply a 'preparation for the gospel', to use a
phrase often applied to it in the Christian tradition. The Old
Testament represents theology in its own right, in the way it speaks
about God, the world and mankind, addressing the issues and
wrestling with the problems of Old Testament times. The New
Testament cannot be used as an absolutely normative key to the Old
Testament. As we saw earlier, the New Testament is the product of
a particular historical period and naturally reflects and reacts to the
concerns of that age. (The treatment of Psalm 110 in St Mark's
Gospel is typical of first-century Jewish exegesis of the Scriptures.)
Truth cannot be conveyed in a cultural vacuum. As we have said,
this should not be a cause of anxiety; it is inevitably true of all
literature and does not prevent us from ascribing a very high degree

of authority to the New Testament writings. It does, however, mean that the New Testament cannot be used as a definitive key to the literature of other ages.

How then might we express the relationship between the Old Testament and the New in a positive way? The relationship is perhaps best thought of as consisting essentially in a great continuity of religious tradition. What we call the Old Testament was the Bible of Jesus and of Paul. When Marcion, in the second century, sought to exclude the Jewish elements from the Bible, he could not rest content with rejecting the Old Testament. He had, as we have seen, to reject large parts of the New Testament as well. In fact, if he had been absolutely consistent, he would have had to reject the whole of the New Testament, for there is virtually nothing in it which does not owe a great deal to the Old Testament and the Judaism which it shaped. The influence of Greek thought in the New Testament is not to be ignored, but it is overwhelmingly in terms of the categories and concepts of the Old Testament that the New Testament authors express themselves. Broad theological concepts first grasped by the theologians of Israel later provide the framework of New Testament thought. For example, the notion of a just and loving God who acts faithfully for his people; the notions of sin and forgiveness—it is very much from the Old Testament tradition that Christianity has inherited these and other basic theological categories. More specifically, the New Testament writers draw on certain key phrases or even institutions of the Old Testament in their attempt to make sense of Jesus' life and death. Titles or phrases such as 'Son of Man', 'Servant' and 'Messiah' (the Hebrew word of which the Greek word 'Christ' is a translation) are reapplied to Jesus, in the difficult task of trying to express his significance. The meanings of these originally distinct and separate Old Testament titles or phrases are often modified considerably in the process of being brought together and reapplied to Jesus, but their origin is unmistakably in the Old Testament. In a similar way, the idea of the important Old Testament institution of temple sacrifice is employed in the New Testament (for example, in the Epistle to the Hebrews) in the attempt to make some sense of Jesus' terrible death.

Thus it was very largely the Old Testament which provided the theological vocabulary which the authors of the New Testament used to express their insights into God's activity in Jesus. These authors had a strong sense of their continuity with Old Testament tradition. Certainly they had experienced a distinctively new and decisive act of God in Jesus, but this was thought of as, in a very important sense, the culmination of God's activity for his people Israel. As we have stressed, the distinctiveness of the New Testament is misunderstood if it is expressed in terms of an exaggerated dichotomy or contrast between the Old Testament and the New. The distinctiveness of the New Testament seems to be in the advent of Jesus as the fulfilment of the aspirations and hopes which are at the very heart of the Old Testament. We must not, of course, forget the serious reservations we have expressed about certain ways of understanding the sense in which the New Testament may be said to fulfil the Old. We have stressed that the New Testament in many cases seems to understand the Old Testament in ways which the original authors probably did not intend, and that in such cases the Old Testament must be allowed to be itself and not be subordinated to the New Testament's understanding of it. Nevertheless, it is possible, without forgetting that the Old Testament authors were men of their time addressing the issues of their own day, for us to claim that the New Testament fulfils the best hopes and aspirations of the Old. The authors of the Old Testament, as they spoke about God's activity in the history of their own day, gave to posterity concepts, vocabulary and above all hopes which proved invaluable to the theologians of the early Church as they sought to give expression to all that they had experienced in Jesus. Moreover, for the Christian, who believes that God was at work in a decisive way in Jesus, and that this is the very same God in whom Israel has always hoped, it is quite fitting to believe that the historical and cultural development which provided the concepts and vocabulary in which the Christ event was expressed by the Church was not arbitrary or accidental, but under the providential guidance of God.

FOR FURTHER READING

A very wide-ranging discussion about the history and problems of the OT in relation to the NT is to be found in D. L. Baker, *Two Testaments, One Bible* (Leicester, Inter-Varsity Press, 1976).

9

Epilogue
Using the Old Testament

JOHN ROGERSON

Many who study the OT do not wish to be content with knowing about it from the literary and historical-critical point of view. They wish to use it in their lives. For those who become full-time workers in the Church, there may be the necessity to preach about the OT or to lead discussion groups on OT books or themes. Those who enter the teaching profession may be expected to know about the ways in which the OT can be applied to social and moral questions.

College and university courses which include the study of the OT often do not cover these matters. Many regard it as the task of theological seminaries to teach such things. There is sometimes a gulf between what is taught academically about the OT, and the use that professional people are expected to make of the OT. Several of the essays in this book have pointed to some of the ways in which the academic foundations for the modern use of the OT can be laid. This Epilogue seeks to address itself more directly to the subject of using the OT.

A   *Using the Old Testament in the Church*

In church services the OT is usually required to play a secondary role to the NT. Whereas books of the NT may be read and preached upon systematically, OT readings are usually chosen because they are thought to illumine or to anticipate the NT readings. An effect of this is that many congregations are not familiar with the OT as a whole, but are fed with a diet of readings gleaned from all over the OT, and have very little idea how these are related. Apart from the chapters of Genesis that deal with creation and 'fall', there may be few passages of the OT that become the subjects of sermons in their own right. References to the OT may often assert what earlier chapters of this book have sought to deny: for example, that the OT presents a God of wrath while the NT presents a God of love; or that the OT is simply a record of religious evolution from primitive and barbaric conceptions of God to something approaching the spirit of the Sermon on the Mount.

One fact that has been constantly stressed in previous chapters is that of *diversity* within the OT. It is precisely this diversity which should be the starting-point for the use of the OT in the Church. The fact is that the OT was produced over such a long period of time and in so many different situations, that there are many circumstances of the religious life of the churches and of individuals today that are paralleled in the OT. The OT is particularly candid about doubt and uncertainty, for example, and in parts of books such as Jeremiah, the Psalms, Job and Ecclesiastes it expresses sentiments that must have occurred to many sensitive Christians today.

At another level, because its historical traditions span such a long stretch of time, it enables us to get a perspective on the interrelationship between God's search for mankind and that confused response of his people that ranges from positive commitment to outright rebellion, via indifference and the desire to use God merely to further human ambitions. Because the story of God's search and the people's response covers so much time, it provides a warning that we should not regard any particular segment of the story as though it were the whole truth. Elijah's complaint that he alone is left of all the servants of God, and even his life is threatened (1 Kings 19.10) is as unrepresentative of the fortunes of the people of God as are those apparent high-points of Israel's history in which zealous kings forced religious compliance upon a reluctant people. The narratives of the ups and downs of the fortunes of the people of God in the OT can help the Church today to set its life in a wider context of the call of God and the responses of the people. It can serve as a corrective to false prophets of doom or prosperity, who deduce from their immediate situations the imminent demise of the Church or the imminent conversion of the world.

One of the most fundamental problems of the Church today (by no means a new problem) is that of the inclusive versus the exclusive Church. This can be illuminated by the OT. The problem is whether the Church should consist only of the totally committed, i.e. be exclusive, or whether it should embrace many members who may never be more than nominal Christians. The OT does not decide in favour of either alternative; rather, it exposes the shortcomings of both positions.

Basically, Israel as the people of God was something inclusive. Membership was a matter of birth, but the existence of the whole people depended upon the grace of God. God had shown that grace supremely in the Exodus deliverance, but also in subsequent dealings with the people. The response to this grace and to membership of the people of God was to be obedience to God's law and covenant (cf. the opening of the Decalogue: 'I am the LORD your God, who brought you out of the land of Egypt . . . you shall have no other gods before me' (Exodus 20.2–3). In the event, the response fell short of what might have been expected. The people turned to other gods; when these failed them, they turned back to God, but they soon forgot him as soon as their immediate problems were solved. Some of the most remarkable illustrations of this type of response are to be found in the traditions about the wilderness wanderings. Here, the very generation that had experienced the deliverance from Egypt behaved so faithlessly, that it was condemned not to enter the promised land, a fate which Moses was also forced to share (cf. Deut. 32.48–52).

The pitfalls of the inclusive view of the people of God are clear. By no means everybody is grateful for unsolicited inclusion in the people of God, with the attendant responsibilities. Unwilling and unco-operative members of the people of God can make life hard for those who are faithful, or for the chosen ministers of God. On the other hand, an inclusive view of the people of God asserts the lordship of God over every aspect of the life of the people, whether they like it or not. Religion is not an affair for the few who like that sort of thing. Religion is an important part of reality, and the faithful must be prepared to suffer on account of, and on behalf of, the unfaithful, as they maintain their vision.

The exclusive view of the people of God is represented, for example, by the post-exilic community in Jerusalem from which were expelled all who were not of proper descent (e.g. Nehemiah 13.23–30). It is often said that the books of Jonah and Ruth, both of which describe the faith of non-Israelites, were written in protest at this exclusivism. Whatever may be the truth of this suggestion, both Ruth and Jonah maintain that the purposes and working of God cannot be confined to the chosen people, let alone to an idealized or exclusive form of the chosen people. An exclusive idea of the people of God may avoid the problem of the half- or non-committed, but it runs the risk of narrowing God's purposes until they concern only the people of God as narrowly defined.

Ancient Israel as the people of God, whether considered inclusively or exclusively, and the Church share the situation that they owe their existence to divine grace in the past, and that they look forward to a consummation in the future. Just because OT hopes are in one sense fulfilled for Christians in the ministry, death and resurrection of Jesus, it must not be overlooked that the Church still looks for a consummation, and that the OT supplies many of the categories in which the NT describes that consummation. The effective acknowledgement by all the nations that God is king is no more complete for the Church than it was for ancient Israel. In spite of God's revelation in Jesus Christ, the Church is no more a willing, dedicated instrument for his purposes than was Israel. Because ancient Israel and the Church both live in the paradox of the already and the not-yet, much material in the OT can provide illumination for church life.

At the level of the individual, the OT contains, especially in its Psalter, the repository of the inspiration, hopes, doubts and fears of generations of believers. In its insights into the heart of mankind, its terminology for wrongdoing is more profound and far-reaching than what is to be found in the NT (cf. Psalm 51). It would do no harm if preachers who speak glibly about 'sin' were to make a careful study of the vocabulary of the OT in the matter of wrongdoing and rebellion against God.

There are no simple hermeneutical rules that can be applied to the OT to make it yield messages for any conceivable situation today. Its use in the Church requires at least the following: (a) knowledge of its whole content; (b) a recognition of its diversity; (c) a readiness to avoid over-simplifying formulae such as that it displays primarily a God of wrath; (d) a willingness to see it as a witness to faith of people who lived in real and often difficult circumstances; (e) a readiness to learn all that is possible from academic and critical scholarship.

Ultimately, such is the diversity of the OT that its use in the Church will be to some extent a personal matter for each serious user. Different users will be drawn to different parts of it, and will apply those parts to their own particular circumstances. The work involved will be considerable, but so are the potential rewards for the Church.

B *Using the Old Testament in Social and Moral Questions*

A feature of current church life is the renewal of interest being shown in all sections of the Church in social and moral issues. In one matter, the OT has moved into a place of prominence, in that the movement known as liberation theology has taken many of its ideas of justice and of salvation from the OT rather than from the NT.

It cannot be said too strongly that those who use the OT in social and moral issues must avoid selectivity; or at any rate, if they use the OT selectively, they must be clear on what grounds they do this. For example, it is all very well to say that Genesis 9.6,

Whoever sheds the blood of man, by man shall his blood be shed.

justifies capital punishment for the crime of murder. But the OT also insists on the death penalty for those who strike or curse their parents (Exodus 21.15, 17) or those who commit homosexual acts (Leviticus 20.13). Those who argue that Genesis 9.6 should be applied to modern society must also make it clear whether they think that the same holds for the passages from Exodus and Leviticus cited above. If they do not think that these passages are applicable, they should state why.

Again, it is customary to use Genesis 2.24,

therefore shall a man leave his parents and cleave to his wife and the two shall become one flesh

to argue that monogamy represents God's purpose in marriage. To be fair, Jesus appears to understand the verse in this way and to give his authority to this interpretation (Matthew 19.4–6). But it ought to be noted that if this is what the writer of Genesis 2.24 intended, there are serious exceptions in the OT which are not condemned on this score. Abraham (if Hagar counts), Jacob, Elkanah (the father of Samuel), David and Solomon had more than one wife at a time. This is not to suggest that Genesis 2.24 cannot, and should not be interpreted as advocating monogamy; it is a plea that this interpretation should not be pressed in isolation from what the OT contains as a whole.

Another example of a text that is often used regardless of the rest of the OT is Genesis 1.27:

> So God created man in his own image, in the image of God he created him; male and female he created them.

It is often argued that this passage asserts the absolute sanctity of human life in God's sight, since men and women are made in his image. Whether or not this is a correct interpretation of this passage, it ought not to be asserted without some attempt being made to come to terms with the fact that in the book of Joshua, God appears to require the killing of all the Canaanites who occupy the promised land (Joshua 10.40). It is difficult to see how it can be maintained that the OT asserts the sanctity of life, if no explanation of the Joshua passages is offered.

The fact is that within the OT, the diversity of material makes it possible to support any number of opposing positions, as John Barton points out in his chapter on Ethics. Those who wish to see revolution against the state might appeal to the fact that Elisha initiated *coups d'état* in both Israel and Syria (2 Kings 8.13; 9.1–3). Those who regard revolution as against the will of God might point to the actions of David. He spared Saul when Saul was in his power, because Saul was God's anointed (1 Samuel 26.8–9), and dealt harshly with those who claimed to have killed Saul and Saul's son (David's rival) Ish baal (2 Samuel 1.14–16; 4.9–12).

In the matter of whether one's duty to one's country comes before duty to one's conscience or religious convictions, Jeremiah might well be quoted on the side of putting religion and conscience first. During the siege of Jerusalem in 588–7 BC, he advocated surrender to the Babylonians. He was accused of undermining the morale of the people, and he was placed under arrest (Jeremiah 38.4–6). Over a century earlier, Isaiah had urged the king to stand fast against the Assyrians who were besieging Jerusalem (2 Kings 19.5–7). Whereas Isaiah saw the deliverance of Jerusalem in 701 BC in terms of God leaving a remnant and not making a complete end of his people (Isaiah 1.9), for Jeremiah, the fall of Jerusalem and the exile of the people did not spell out the end of God's dealings with his people (Jeremiah 32.42–4). This latter example is interesting in the light of the current debate about whether the occupation of the

West by communism is such a terrible prospect, that any means, including nuclear war, are justifiable to prevent it.

There are, however, matters on which a much greater measure of agreement can be found in the OT. The perversion of justice and the denial of rights to the weak and to the poor are condemned throughout the OT. The duty of the strong to support and to protect the weak is stressed. Above all, appeal is made to God's grace in redeeming his people as the ground for gracious treatment of others. In the Deuteronomic version of the Ten Commandments (Deuteronomy 5.12–15), the redemption from slavery in Egypt is the reason why a man's servants must rest on the Sabbath as well as himself. In the Deuteronomic regulations about releasing slaves after they have served for seven years, the Exodus deliverance is the ground for generous treatment of slaves when they are released.

The treatment of the female slave in Deuteronomy 15 is an interesting case that may provide one of the most useful clues to using the OT in social and moral issues. If Deuteronomy 15.12ff is compared with Exodus 21.7–11 (whose exact translation and interpretation are not free from problems—see the standard commentaries), it seems likely that in Deuteronomy 15, female slaves are treated more favourably than in Exodus 21. Indeed, in Deuteronomy 15.12, the reference to the female slave seems to be a subsequent addition to the text. If it is a subsequent addition, this is most important. It shows us a process at work within the formation of the OT tradition whereby the OT principles of justice based upon the graciousness of God are extended to include new classes of people, in this case, female slaves.

In the light of this, we might say that the use of the OT in social and moral questions is not a matter of quoting texts and of applying them to modern situations. It is a matter of discovering the dominant social and moral imperatives of the OT and of working them out in terms of the needs that are disclosed to us by our moral sensitivity in the world today. The OT was not intended to be a book of rules applicable in any conceivable situation. It is, among other things, the record of a growing sensitivity to the social and moral demands implicit in the gracious redemption of God. That growth in moral sensitivity has continued to our own day. For example, the OT (and the NT!) takes slavery for granted; we have abolished it. Yet the paradox remains that for all our growth in moral sensitivity, we still succeed in denying justice in the world, and in devising sophisticated techniques for destroying or de-humanizing the human race. The growth in moral sensitivity does not mean that a little more education will bring about the perfection of the world. It indicates that the modern world is as much in need as ever of the OT visions and hopes of a world restored, and of loyalty to the God who alone can work the restoration. In our own situation, the OT provides us with clues and challenges about the justice which God desires and which the world needs. We are called to work out the implications of these clues and challenges for ourselves in the modern world.

Index